SUNSET
BOULEVARD

FROM MOVIE
TO MUSICAL

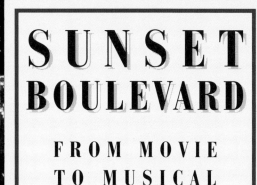

SUNSET
BOULEVARD

FROM MOVIE
TO MUSICAL

GEORGE PERRY

FOREWORD BY
ANDREW LLOYD WEBBER

AN OWL BOOK

HENRY HOLT AND COMPANY
NEW YORK

Henry Holt and Company, Inc.
Publishers since 1866
115 West 18th Street
New York, New York 10011

Henry Holt ® is a registered
trademark of Henry Holt and Company, Inc.

First published in the United States in 1993 by
Henry Holt and Company, Inc.
Originally published in Great Britain in 1993 by
PAVILION BOOKS LTD.

Library of Congress Catalog Card Number: 93-78558

ISBN 0-8050-2927-3

Henry Holt books are available for special promotions and
premiums. For details contact: Director, Special Markets.

First American Edition - 1993

Designed by Bridgewater Books

Printed in Great Britain
All first editions are printed on acid-free paper. ∞

1 3 5 7 9 10 8 6 4 2
Special photography by Donald Cooper, David Crosswaite and
Tony McGee.

CONTENTS

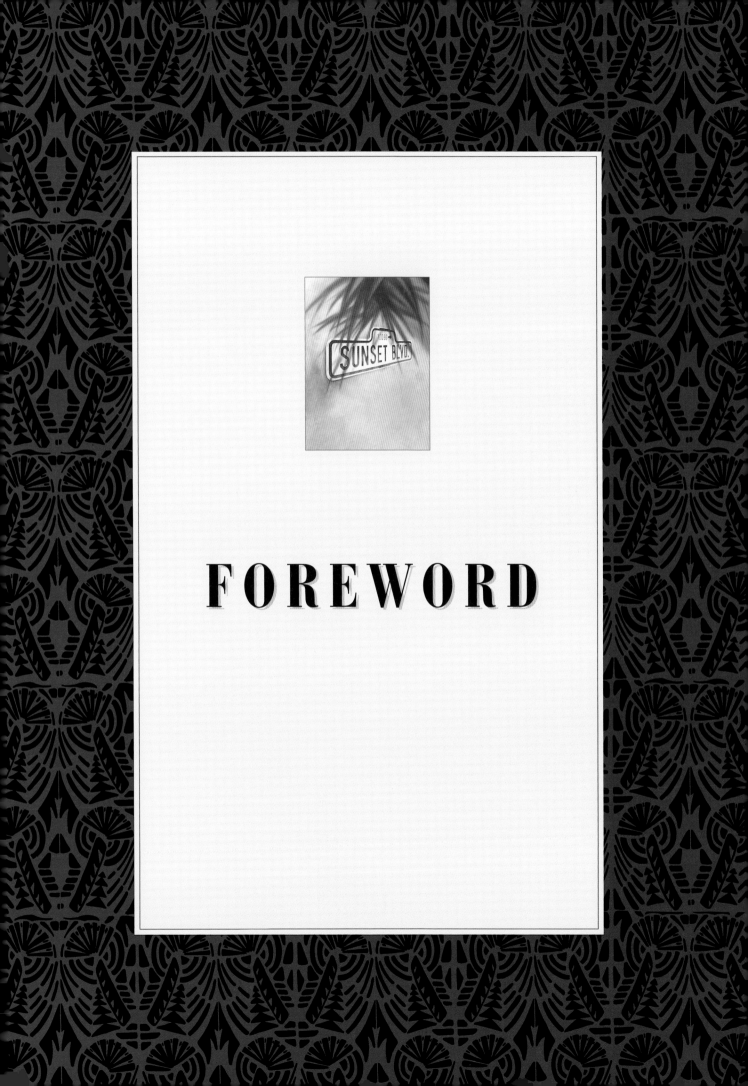

FOREWORD

INSPIRED BY
SUNSET BOULEVARD

I first saw *Sunset Boulevard* at some time during the early 1970s. It made such an impression on me that it inspired a tune that I felt could be the title song. Unfortunately, I neither had the rights to the film, nor was I at that time likely to obtain them. However, I eventually used a couple of fragments of that tune in Stephen Frears' affectionate Bogie spoof, *Gumshoe*.

In 1976 Hal Prince began working with me on the musical *Evita*. We discussed *Sunset Boulevard* and I saw the movie again because Hal had obtained the rights. It all came to nothing, but I remember coming up with an idea for the moment when Norma Desmond returns to Paramount Studios.

At around that period I had a meeting with Christopher Hampton whom I had known for some years because he was at school with Tim Rice. Chris had already declared an interest in writing the libretto of *Sunset Boulevard* for the English National Opera, but again nothing resulted. We thought it was a wonderful idea but reached the conclusion that in both our cases other projects we were working on made *Sunset* impossible at that time, and there was still the matter of whether or not we would acquire the rights.

On and off for the next twelve years I thought of *Sunset*. It was only after *Aspects of Love*, however, that I felt it was the subject I had to compose next.

I contacted Paramount and this time the rights were available. So I took an option and began work. As is always the case, several early jottings were discarded. Then I remembered Chris Hampton's interest. He was intrigued but felt that he would be happier if he could work with someone who had experience of lyric writing. So I introduced him to my old friend and collaborator Don Black, and what I had hoped most to happen would seem to have done so. With great success they collaborated on both the book and the lyrics.

I began composing the score shortly after the opening of *Aspects of Love* in London in 1989. Having tried various versions of the title song I came back to the original idea that I first had in the early 1970s, albeit in a very different style and form. For the moment when Norma returns to Paramount I stayed with my late seventies draft, and with it came 'As If We Never Said Goodbye'. Otherwise, mostly everything in my version of *Sunset Boulevard*, as described in this book, has been written since 1989.

POSTSCRIPT

As with any new musical, *Sunset* is still an evolving animal. Already several changes have been made in London. Now the Los Angeles production gives us all a chance to put other ideas into practice. This is the exciting part of a new production. Our Los Angeles cast includes Glenn Close as Norma and George Hearn as Max. I can't wait to see what our LA cast brings to the party.

SIR ANDREW LLOYD WEBBER OCTOBER 1993

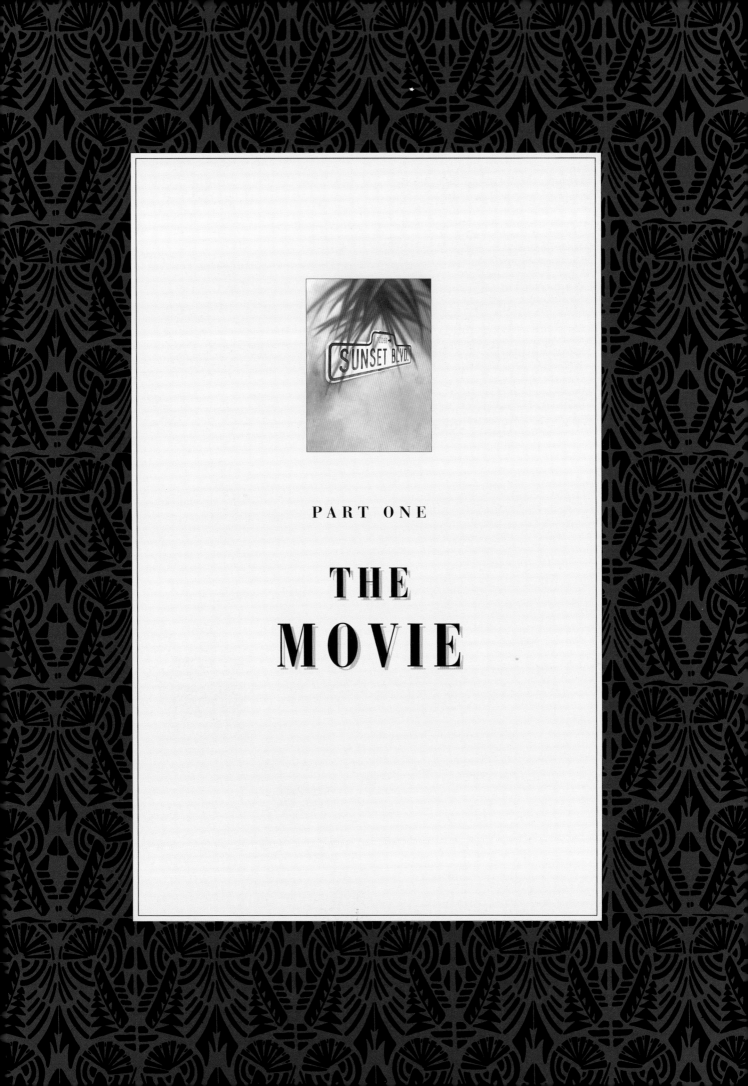

PART ONE

THE
MOVIE

Where does Sunset Boulevard begin? Surprisingly, the thoroughfare so closely associated with Hollywood actually starts in the oldest quarter of Los Angeles, almost at the geographical point where the first settlement took root in the 18th century. Since 1939 the Union Station, constructed as the terminal for the Southern Pacific, Union Pacific and Santa Fé railroads, and one of the most handsome buildings of modern Los Angeles, has stood on the site. In front of the station is the Plaza, a tiny circular park with a delicate, almost dainty bandstand in its middle. It is the earliest public space of El Pueblo de la Reina de Los Angeles, and around it the first fourteen families from the Mission San Gabriel Archangel built their homes on the banks of the Porciuncula River, following orders from the Spanish governor in 1781.

◆

BELOW LOS ANGELES AS SURVEYED IN 1849.
THE AS YET UNNAMED SUNSET BOULEVARD IGNORES
THE NEW STREET GRID AS IT SKIRTS
THE FOOTHILLS ON ITS ROUTE NORTH-WEST.

ABOVE THE PLAZA, IN THE OLDEST QUARTER OF LOS ANGELES, AROUND 1850. IT IS CLOSE TO THIS POINT THAT SUNSET BOULEVARD BEGINS ITS TWENTY-SEVEN MILE LENGTH.

From there Sunset Boulevard, its ancient origin a simple cow trail that led from the byre to a nearby hillside pasture, commences its serpentine progress of twenty-seven miles into the west. (For much of its distance Sunset Boulevard ignores the familiar grid pattern of city streets, curving at will, to follow the topography of the hills and ravines along its route as it skirts the southern slopes of the Santa Monica Mountains.)

Through Hollywood the road flows, past the gaudy Strip with its cafés, nightspots and gigantic billboards, through the sedate residential calm of Beverly Hills, into the Westside and along the northern flank of the

campus of the University of California at Los Angeles (UCLA). It passes over the San Diego freeway to Brentwood, and it makes its descent around the southern tip of the Will Rogers State Historic Park, finally coming to an end at Pacific Palisades on the Pacific Coast Highway between Santa Monica and Malibu. Facing it is the awesome natural boundary of the ocean.

Sunset Boulevard. It is a name that resonates throughout the world as a symbol of Hollywood, although the film capital is just one of the five communities it traverses. In a sense Sunset Boulevard epitomizes the aspirant spirit of America; it climbs out of a dense inner-city area populated by immigrants, ascends the social ladder up to the sumptuous homes of Beverly Hills billionaires, then continues to its nirvana – a golden sunset blazing over the Pacific Ocean.

The modest cow trail began its transformation into an urban street in the middle of the nineteenth century, after the ending of California's Mexican rule. Los Angeles was already the largest town in the western republic, its *rancheros* wealthy from trade with the *Yanquis*, and from supplying meat and hides to the optimistic fortune seekers, the Forty-Niners, who had migrated to take their chances in the Californian gold rush. Later came the Chinese, many of them retired from working mines in the Mojave desert or northern California. They began to colonize alongside the established Mexicans. The road linked their two communities, with the old Chinatown remaining intact right up until the

Union Station was built. The modern Los Angeles Chinatown was then established on North Broadway.

After the Civil War settlers from the east poured into the expanding southern Californian metropolis, and the street began to make its way towards the foothills. The Southern Pacific's transcontinental railroad opened in 1869. Following the establishment of a rival link by the Santa Fé railroad, a land boom turned Los Angeles into the fastest-growing city in the world. The evocative, inspirational street name, initially Sunset Avenue, appears to have been coined by an unknown, but indisputably imaginative municipal worker around 1888, and it begins to be named on maps from that time. By now

◆

BELOW A LATE 19TH-CENTURY VIEW OF HOLLYWOOD ORANGE GROVES. THE RANCHER IN THE FOREGROUND IS STANDING CLOSE TO THE PRESENT-DAY INTERSECTION OF SUNSET AND GOWER.

ABOVE SUNSET BOULEVARD IS STILL A RURAL
DIRT ROAD IN 1905 AS IT PASSES THE
FARM BUILDINGS OF HOLLYWOOD. THE CHILDREN
ARE STANDING AT THE GOWER CROSSING.

the city engineers were imposing the new road across the existing street grid, demolishing properties that stood in the way. The Los Angeles County Railroad laid tracks west along it. Behind a quaint steam locomotive, its boiler enclosed within glazed coachwork, was pulled a standard railroad car.

The history of Los Angeles in the last 100 years is written on Sunset Boulevard. Within recent living memory the downtown area of the city has been transformed. It is now girdled by a network of freeways, the first of which, the Pasadena, did not open until 1940. Since the 1950s awkward hills have been flattened into oblivion and decrepit old buildings replaced by the soaring high-rises that only became permissible after the

easing of the earthquake code. Apart from the impressive art deco City Hall (built in 1928) a thirteen-storey limit was maintained until 1957. Olvera Street, at right angles to Sunset near the Plaza, has become the touristic Mexican quarter, a picturesque enclave in stark contrast to other Latino areas of the central city.

It is the start of Sunset's ascent to the demographically mixed neighbourhood of Echo Park, formerly known as Edendale, passing the huge temple built by the evangelist Aimee Semple Macpherson in the 1920s, and still in use today. At Virgil Avenue, Hollywood Boulevard begins, Sunset veering to the left. Then comes the straightest stretch of Sunset as it runs parallel with Hollywood Boulevard for over four-and-a-half miles, before reaching the irregular undulations of the Strip.

Hollywood had been given its name by the wife of Harvey H Wilcox, a property

BEGINNINGS

ABOVE HARVEY H WILCOX, THE KANSAS
PROHIBITIONIST WHO IN THE 1870S BOUGHT LAND
WEST OF ECHO PARK. ABOVE HIM IS HIS WIFE
DAEIDA WHO NAMED THE ACREAGE HOLLYWOOD.

the name, which she had heard applied to an estate in Illinois. Wilcox prospered, and in 1887 he subdivided his property, mapping out the streets north of Sunset including what was then called Prospect Avenue, but would in time become Hollywood Boulevard. The only place his name is commemorated today is Wilcox Avenue, one of the cross streets of Hollywood and Sunset Boulevards.

The early community, with its houses sprinkled among the orange groves, was quiet and conservative, a haven for retired mid-westerners and a few farmers, separated from the fast-growing city of Los Angeles by several miles of dirt road. Three factors brought about the transformation of the sleepy, well-ordered township, incorporated as a city in 1903 although the population was then only around 700, into modern Hollywood. First, its annexation by the city of Los Angeles, welcomed because it brought with it a proper water supply. Secondly, the construction downtown of the Hill Street tunnel for the Pacific Electric Railway with its fast, red trolley cars, the precursor of the freeway system, which brought it well within the commuter belt. Finally, there was the advent of Hollywood's very own industry; the movies.

The first film pioneers arrived in the then peaceful area as early as 1907 with the intention of taking advantage of the hours of sunshine and constant clement weather (film stages then were usually in the open-air) and a comfortable distance from the attentions of the monopolistic Motion Picture Patents Company, later known as the Edison Trust. The MPPC employed ruthless methods against anyone using, but not paying royalties on the camera mechanism. In a questionable

developer and fervent prohibitionist from Kansas, who had bought land three miles west of Echo Park in the 1870s in order to farm it with citrus fruits, beans and cucumbers. Holly, however, was not indigenous and was resistant to all attempts to introduce it, but Wilcox's wife, Daeida, liked the sound of

ABOVE LOOKING SOUTH ACROSS
HOLLYWOOD BOULEVARD IN 1905. SUNSET
RUNS PARALLEL IN THE DISTANCE. ONLY
THE BUILDING IN THE IMMEDIATE
FOREGROUND STILL STANDS.

courtroom decision it had been deemed to
have been invented by Thomas Alva Edison.

In 1907, the Selig company from
Chicago made a ten-minute version of *The
Count of Monte Cristo* on a stage built behind
the Sing Loo Chinese laundry in downtown
Los Angeles. It was the first film to be made
in southern California. In the following year
Colonel Selig built a studio in Edendale, fol-
lowed by the Bison company in 1909, and in
1910 D W Griffith, who had made over 400
short films for Biograph, most of them in
New York, arrived to revel in the crisp, clear
Californian light.

ABOVE THE BIG RED CARS OF THE
PACIFIC ELECTRIC RAILWAY BROUGHT HOLLYWOOD
WITHIN A FEW MINUTES OF DOWNTOWN
LOS ANGELES AFTER THE HILL STREET TUNNEL
WAS OPENED.

ABOVE THE ABANDONED BLONDEAU TAVERN AT SUNSET AND GOWER, WHICH HAD BEEN CLOSED BY
PROHIBITIONISTS, BECAME THE FIRST FILM STUDIO IN HOLLYWOOD IN 1911.

Many of the first studios were on or close to Sunset Boulevard, such as Nestor, Mutual, Kinemacolor, Griffith-Fine Arts, Selig, Keystone, Biograph and Mabel Normand. Nestor was the first, having begun in the old and disused Blondeau tavern (which had been closed by the prohibitionists) and its outhouses on the corner of Sunset and Gower. It was the very site that Columbia would occupy for decades, becoming known as Gower Gulch on account of the cowboys who would hang around hoping for film jobs. Without the frequent interruptions to production by bad weather that had been the bane of filmmaking at their former base in New Jersey, Nestor was soon making three short movies a week, mostly westerns.

The constant sunshine was matched by the availability of low-priced labour, and the filmmakers quickly found that their production costs were halved from those that prevailed in New York. It was in New York, however, that the business side of the industry remained, close to the money market, even though it was a four-day train journey away from Los Angeles, and no transcontinental telephone link would exist until 1915. The coast-to-coast gap between production and financial management has in most cases remained ever since.

So many studios began to open that the Hollywood municipal authorities enacted a zoning law, which is why the studios are dispersed over a wide swathe of the west Los Angeles conurbation. Extending from Universal, beyond the Cahuenga pass at Lankershim, and Warner Brothers and Disney at Burbank, the industry stretches even further into the San Fernando Valley to Culver City near the Baldwyn Hills in the south, where Metro-Goldwyn-Mayer, Selznick International and Hal Roach studios would be located.

In 1913 Cecil B DeMille arrived in California with his partners, Jesse Lasky and Samuel Goldfish (who later changed his name to Goldwyn). They had been attempting to shoot a western in Flagstaff, Arizona. DeMille, directing his first film, was already a master of the profligate grand gesture. In his autobiography he says that he decided, when he got to Arizona, that it did not look like Wyoming, where the story was set. So, he hustled his partners and the crew back aboard the train for southern California. Jesse Lasky in his account suggests that a more pertinent reason was that they came to Flagstaff during a fierce civil war between the cattlemen and the sheepmen. DeMille had heard that conditions in Los Angeles were good for filmmakers and that the thugs hired by the Patents Company would be left even further behind. And indeed, should sudden flight become necessary the Mexican border was only a relatively short distance away.

The newcomers rented half of a large horse barn a few hundred yards north of Sunset on the corner of

◆

Selma and Vine, and it became the studio in which they made the western they had aborted in Arizona. *The Squaw Man* became the first full-length feature to be wholly shot in Hollywood. DeMille and Lasky, with foresight, had the barn moved to the backlot of Paramount Studios in 1927 where for many years its exterior would often appear in westerns. The inside was turned into the studio gym in which stars would work off surplus pounds. In 1979 Paramount gave the wooden structure, by then designated a California Historic Landmark, to the Hollywood Chamber of Commerce who had it restored and moved to its present position near the Hollywood Bowl. The film city's oldest studio building now functions as a museum honouring silent movies.

RIGHT SHORTLY BEFORE IT WAS MOVED TO THE PARAMOUNT STUDIOS, THE BARN WHERE *THE SQUAW MAN* WAS MADE THIRTEEN YEARS EARLIER, IN 1913 IS CONTEMPLATED BY JESSE LASKY.

Moving pictures had drawn their early audiences from fairground sideshows, vaudeville interludes, and nickelodeon peepshows in hastily converted shops. They now began to be presented in dedicated theatres, with audiences expecting greater comfort and value for money. Films went from being regarded as an entertaining novelty to becoming the sensation of the twentieth century, and the name of Hollywood resounded throughout the world, as people in almost every country flocked to the new cinemas that were opening up. Immigrant entrepreneurs migrated to California to make the most of a new industry in which there was no tradition of expertise. There was Louis B Mayer from Minsk, Lewis J Selznick from Kiev, Carl Laemmle from Laupheim, Samuel Goldwyn from Warsaw and Adolph Zukor from Hungary. There were also native-born Americans such as Jesse Lasky from San Francisco, Thomas Ince from Newport, Rhode Island and David Wark Griffith from La Grange, Kentucky. These were the men who turned the carnival attraction into a great American industry.

Ince had begun making films on a 20,000 acre ranch meeting the ocean at Pacific Palisades, where he built a studio known as Inceville. He engaged an entire Wild West show consisting of authentic cowboys and Sioux Indians, horses and buffalo herds, to give a sense of realism and spectacle to the westerns he was shooting. In 1915

BEGINNINGS

BELOW SUNSET AND GOWER BECAME KNOWN LATER
AS GOWER GULCH, A HANG-OUT FOR HOPEFUL
COWBOYS TRYING FOR JOBS IN WESTERNS MADE BY
THE POVERTY ROW STUDIOS.

Ince, D W Griffith and Mack Sennett joined forces to form the Triangle Company, and began construction of the studios at Culver City that were to become famous as the home of Metro-Goldwyn-Mayer, and are now owned by the Sony Corporation for Columbia.

In 1910 the star system had been instigated by Carl Laemmle when he enticed Florence Lawrence, who had been known simply as the Biograph girl, to join his newly formed Independent Motion Picture Company of America (IMP). By means of publicity

BELOW THE OLD TAVERN, TRANSFORMED IN 1911
TO THE FLOURISHING NESTOR STUDIO,
MAKING THREE PICTURES A WEEK.

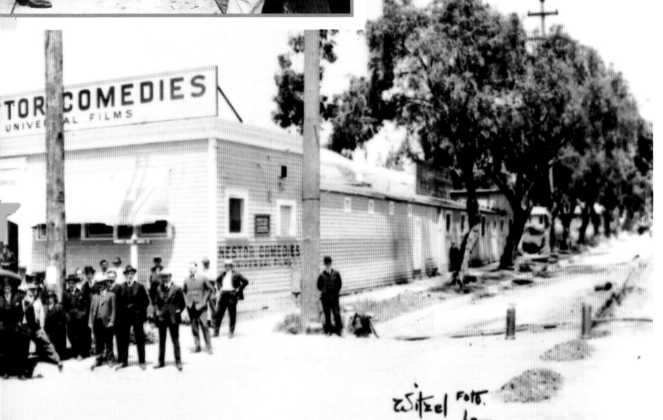

stunts he ensured that the public knew her name. Stardom was born.

Soon audiences were eager to identify their favourites, who were then deluged with fan mail. Stardom brought huge incomes in its wake for some. In 1916 an English comedian who had first toured American vaudeville houses five years earlier with the Fred Karno troupe, and had now become the most famous man in the world, signed a contract with Mutual that provided him with $670,000 for a year's work, a salary of unprecedented munificence at a time when the average wage was around $10 a week. Charles Chaplin was then twenty-six years old. In the following year a tiny Canadian actress born as Gladys Smith, but who became Mary Pickford, and had started at Biograph on $40 a week, was earning $350,000 per film.

During the First World War the American film industry, now securely established on the west coast, took advantage of the turmoil that had severely restricted production in Europe, and surged ahead, quickly dominating the global market. The problems of language were negligible in the silent movie era, mime being a universal tongue, and American films saturated the world's screens. Within five years the formerly languid town in the orange groves had been transformed into a bustling industrial centre, with dozens of movie studios and their ancillary services having sprung up, and its streets were thronged with eager aspirants from all over America seeking work.

It was a boom town. On a site near the intersection of Hollywood and Sunset Boulevards even Babylon was built. In 1915

D W Griffith's controversial historical saga of the American civil war and its aftermath, *The Birth of a Nation*, had ignited the possibilities of the feature film. He strived to make an even more ambitious epic, *Intolerance*. His gigantic Babylonian set towered more than 150 feet above the single-storey wooden houses of East Hollywood and was regarded as the eighth wonder of the world by sightseers, and as a dangerous hazard by the local fire department.

Unhampered by the cumbersome equipment that would arrive with sound, silent moviemakers often used parts of Hollywood and its environs as locations. The chase became a staple of screen comedy; invariably it took place on the streets, thoroughly greased beforehand, with under-cranked cameras capturing in speeded-up motion the antics of Buster Keaton, Charlie Chaplin, the Keystone Kops in their overflowing wagon, Larry Semon, Chester Conklin and the other clowns of the silent screen, including the sublime partnership of Laurel and Hardy.

To gain an idea of what the area looked like in the time of the silent film one only has to look at a few Mack Sennett comedies. In the backgrounds cheap, flimsy buildings line long, straight streets festooned with wires and cables strung from crude wooden poles; the young palms and pepper trees and the grassy sidewalks of residential roads; the big streetcars presenting hazards to drivers of Model T Fords; the clear air, still unhazy from the almost perpetual smog that today engulfs the Los Angeles basin.

West of Fairfax Avenue in the early 1920s Sunset Boulevard was as yet unpaved, although it had now become the principal

ABOVE BY 1935 THE BEVERLY HILLS HOTEL HAD BECOME
A WORLD-FAMOUS LANDMARK OF THE WEALTHIEST AMERICAN CITY.

connection between the centre of Hollywood and Beverly Hills, the pleasant city founded by Burton E Green in 1907 on the site of an earlier, failed township called Morocco. In 1912 the Beverly Hills Hotel had opened its doors, a pink building in Spanish mission style with separate bungalows in its grounds, which had risen up in isolation among the open beanfields. Facing it across Sunset Boulevard a landscaped park with lawns, flowerbeds, shady walks and ponds was created and originally formed part of the hotel premises. Today it is a public open space, named in 1952 after the popular homespun

comedian of the 1920s, Will Rogers. The proprietors of the Beverly Hills Hotel, the Rodeo Land and Water Company, lured Margaret Anderson, the area's most successful hotelier, from the Hollywood Hotel. This had been the area's first luxury establishment, built in the Mission Revival style on the corner of Hollywood Boulevard and Highland Avenue in 1903 when the street was still called Prospect Avenue, and remained there long after its glory had faded until 1956. Mrs Anderson brought to Beverly Hills many of her staff but more significantly, she also brought her clientele, and the empty building lots in the proximity of the new hotel soared in price. The city, which had resisted annexation by Los Angeles, was set on its course to becoming the wealthiest in the United States.

The Pacific Electric Railway had proposed to run a line along Sunset to the sea at Santa Monica, but only a small narrow gauge section was ever opened, intended to provide a shuttle service to the Beverly Trolley Depot a mile to the south. With the growth of automobile traffic following the First World War it proved unprofitable. After its abandonment Mrs Anderson suggested that a bridle path should run down the broad central reservation which had been earmarked for the Pacific Electric tracks. Flanked by flowering

shrubs and surfaced with granite chips, it was to offer the promise of access on horseback to the sea and the mountains via connecting trails. The bridle path actually managed to survive until after the Second World War. Car traffic on Sunset by then had become too heavy and speedy to be impeded by strings of crossing horses, and so the horse track was eventually grassed over.

By the early 1920s street vendors were already peddling their legendarily inaccurate maps of movie stars' homes to gullible tourists, who were conducted in open coaches around the tree-lined streets of Beverly Hills, accompanied by guides with megaphones pointing out who lived where. In the early days of Hollywood the people who worked in films had lived relatively modestly, usually close to their workplace, in order to be ready for the early call and a long day's filming.

BELOW IN THE 1920S A BRIDLE PATH RAN ALONG THE CENTRAL RESERVATION OF SUNSET BOULEVARD THROUGH BEVERLY HILLS. HEAVY POST-WAR TRAFFIC BROUGHT ABOUT ITS REMOVAL.

ABOVE THE SUNSET STRIP IN 1949 –
WHEN SUNSET BOULEVARD WAS MADE.
THIS VIEW IS LOOKING OUT EAST FROM
SAN VICENTE BOULEVARD.

Even Chaplin, on his astronomical salary, initially lived in a succession of small hotels before he acquired his first house.

The earlier stars' homes were in Hollywood itself, or in the Edendale, Los Feliz and Silverlake districts, before the drift began westward. They were often unassuming wood-framed bungalows in the traditional southern Californian style, or small apartment buildings, usually constructed around an inner courtyard. In some parts there was resentment from the established, conservative residents of the old Hollywood who regarded the influx of film industry people with distaste, and froze them out. The shameful sign: 'No Jews, actors or dogs allowed' could sometimes be seen adorning apartment entrances, an indication of the essential provincialism of the place. The exclusive Garden Court on Hollywood Boulevard, the most opulent of the new residential complexes, attempted for many years to exclude any potential tenants connected with the movies unless, as in the case of the producer J Stuart Blackton, they had British accents.

It became necessary for the industry to do its own colonizing. In a sense, the emergence of the architecturally extravagant and luxuriously decorated and furnished movie star home was a consequence of the star system itself, with fans demanding to be impressed by the lifestyle of their idols. For the real estate developers it was a golden era. New roads entered the foothills, winding through the canyons, with lavish properties springing up on virgin hilltops that had been levelled and landscaped. It was possible in an age unfettered by planning restrictions to build in any style, and Moorish castles vied with Tudor mansions, Italian palazzos stood next to Tyrolean lodges. Swimming pools and tennis courts were status symbols that had to be incorporated ingeniously to make the most

BELOW SUNSET AND VINE STREET
IN EARLY POST-WAR YEARS.
LOOKING NORTH FROM VINE STREET
TOWARD HOLLYWOOD BOULEVARD.

ABOVE FALCON LAIR, RUDOLPH VALENTINO'S HOME OVERLOOKING BENEDICT CANYON.

of the steep topography. On the slopes of Mount Lee overlooking the growing town a developer, Harry Chandler, erected a huge sign with individual letters 50 feet high and 30 feet wide. It read 'HOLLYWOODLAND', the name of the 500-acre subdivision. Visible for many miles, at night it was illuminated by 4,000 light bulbs. By the Second World War it had been vandalized and abandoned, and some of the letters had collapsed. But attempts to demolish the eyesore were resisted, and the Hollywood Chamber of Commerce removed the last four letters, eventually refurbishing the sign so that today it is like a Brobdingnagian label for the area, distinctly visible to passengers on the right-hand side of aircraft as they descend into Los Angeles International Airport.

The most celebrated residence was that of Mary Pickford, who had become known as the 'World's Sweetheart', and her husband, the athletic superstar, Douglas Fairbanks.

They were the most famous and the most popular married couple in America. At their home on Summit Drive, an L-shaped Tudor-style mansion which a reporter had named Pickfair, they received not only the most distinguished names in Hollywood but also visiting arts celebrities, world statesmen and European royalty. It was by following the precedent set by Doug and Mary, as the public knew them, that many of the stars, formerly resident in older parts of Hollywood, began to migrate to Beverly Hills. The comedian Harold Lloyd established a huge estate on the county line called Green Acres with a renaissance-style house that possessed twenty-six bathrooms. Chaplin, who also owned a mansion in the grounds of his production centre on Sunset and La Brea, built another on Summit Drive, using carpenters on the studio payroll. It became renowned for its lack of staying power during storms, acquiring the nickname Breakaway House.

Rudolph Valentino, the greatest romantic star of the 1920s chose as his ideal to live in a large, isolated estate called Falcon Lair, high up in Benedict Canyon, to which he moved in 1925, after the break-up of his marriage to Natacha Rambova. His was one of the most extravagant of film-star homes, awash with oriental carpets, renaissance art and medieval armour. The twisting drive would in the 1920s have been dangerous at certain times of the year, and was inaccessible to the tourist buses, if not to the star's cream-coloured Mercedes with its silver cobra radiator cap. Valentino, unfortunately, had very little time to appreciate the attractions of his eyrie. On 23 August 1926 he died from peritonitis, at the age of thirty-one; a tragedy that provoked grief and considerable outbreaks of mass hysteria among his followers world-wide.

In spite of a private life that has been subjected to biographical sensationalism, it would be a mistake to underestimate Valentino's importance as a star. The film historian, Kevin Brownlow, presented a pristine, tinted print of *The Four Horsemen of the Apocalypse* to London audiences in the winter of 1992, and young women, whose grandmothers were not even born when Valentino died, nonetheless found his screen persona electric and compelling, and still capable of generating shock waves of sexual excitement.

A famous sequence in Rex Ingram's 1921 film has Valentino in gaucho garb dancing the tango in an Argentinian café. It became a dance craze, and no home of a star of stature could be without a tiled tango floor. The implication was that the owner was on the Rudy circuit, and were he to drop in, suitable facilities awaited him.

It is hard in the present age of multimedia saturation to appreciate just how renowned movie stars were in that pre-television age. Today's superstars such as Madonna or Michael Jackson are never likely to enjoy the same universal adulation that was accorded Pickford and Fairbanks, Chaplin and Valentino. Millions all over the world followed their progress, informed by extensive newspaper coverage, syndicated gossip columns and large-circulation fan magazines. Studios were unstinting in the resources lavished on their publicity and promotion departments.

The stars influenced the fashion industry, which geared itself to the rapid mass-production of chain-store copies of film-style fashions, enabling every office girl to adopt the look of her favourite star. The cinema became a fashion designer's medium, and little expense was spared on important films to ensure that the stars were seen in breathtaking creations. One of the first to appreciate their impact was Cecil B DeMille, who invited the Paris couturier Paul Iribe to design Gloria Swanson's outfits for *Male and Female* in 1919. One dress was made entirely of pearls, crowned with a jewelled white peacock's head displaying an extravagance of egret feathers. 'No peacock is safe around DeMille' was a Hollywood quip.

The cosmetics industry was another Hollywood by-product. The first make-up department had been set up at the Selig studio in 1917 by George Westmore. He was the founder of a dynasty; all six of his sons were to become eminent at the major studios. Max Factor had arrived in Los Angeles in 1908 and by 1914 had created the first cream

make-up specifically designed for film. Until then only crude stage greasepaint sticks had been used. Factor products developed for films, such as eyeshadow, eyebrow pencils, blenders, powder brushes and lipsticks, were quickly transformed into consumer products. Cosmetics counters appeared in virtually every department store in the world. A multi-million dollar consumer industry had come about as a direct consequence of the movies.

Gloria Swanson, one of the greatest stars of the silent cinema, lived from 1920 for many years in a twenty-two room Italian mansion surrounded by acacias and palms that stood on Sunset Boulevard at Crescent Drive close to the Beverly Hills Hotel, and had

ABOVE GLORIA SWANSON'S OWN ITALIANATE MANSION, OVERLOOKING SUNSET BOULEVARD IN BEVERLY HILLS. SHE LIVED HERE FROM 1920, DURING HER HEYDAY AS A SILENT MOVIE STAR.

been built by King Gillette, the founder of the razor company. Its new owner was twenty-three years old when she bought the property, and she promptly installed a golden tub in her black marble bathroom. At her dinner parties a liveried footman was positioned behind every guest at table, an extravagance she had copied from Buckingham Palace.

Swanson was born in Chicago in 1897 to a Swedish-Italian father and Polish-Alsatian mother. In 1916 she had arrived in Hollywood with the first of her six husbands,

See, Dad, what a big girl you have.

team of Mack Sennett Bathing Beauties for publicity stills advertising *A Pullman Bride*. Contrary to the popular mythology, she was never one of the Bathing Beauties herself and maintained until the end of her life that she had not even learned to swim. Being photographed in a swimsuit and required to cuddle up on the beach to the comedian Mack Swain finally finished her for the chaotic slapstick world of banana skins and custard pies, and it was the last of her films for Sennett. After a brief spell at Triangle, her first big opportunity was given to her by Cecil B DeMille in 1919 when he cast her as the lead in *Don't Change Your Husband*.

DeMille was a shrewd judge of the indefinable presence that went with stardom. He had seen Swanson in a Mack Sennett comedy, investing the simple act of leaning against a door with authority as well as beauty. In mock self-deprecation he said of her: 'The public, not I, made Gloria Swanson a star.' Even so, it was he who coaxed her in the right direction, ensuring that she was seen in extravagant outfits that would catch the eyes of fashion editors, and she became the epitome of Hollywood glamour. Swanson's career at Paramount, the studio that had been born out of the partnership of Jesse Lasky and Adolph Zukor in 1916, was phenomenal. Every year until 1927 when she left Paramount for United Artists, the company founded in 1919 by Chaplin, Fairbanks, Pickford and Griffith, she was their top star at the box office. She made films for Sam Wood, Allan Dwan and others, and a total of six for DeMille. *Male and Female* was a fanciful Hollywood version of J M Barrie's play, *The Admirable Crichton*, which included a

the actor Wallace Beery, to whom she was married for only a few weeks before separating. She had begun her career two years earlier as an extra at the Essanay studios in Chicago, even appearing in an unbilled role as a stenographer in a Chaplin two-reeler called *His New Job*. However, Chaplin had rejected her for a leading part because he felt that she lacked comedy spirit. In Hollywood, Beery signed a contract with Mack Sennett and insisted that his wife also be hired. Subsequently she appeared in several romantic comedies with Bobby Vernon. She was photographed in a swimsuit with the famous dream sequence in which she was pawed by a lion. Another of her DeMille films was *The Affairs of Anatol*, a sophisticated bedroom drama in which she played opposite the tragic morphine-addicted star, Wallace Reid, who died scandalously shortly afterwards.

After a spell in France making *Madame Sans-Gêne*, a story of a laundress during the French Revolution, she came back to Hollywood in triumph in 1925 with her third husband, the Marquis Henri de la Falaise, having cabled ahead: 'Am arriving with the Marquis tomorrow. Please arrange ovation.' Paramount was happy to oblige. Soon after her return, Adolph Zukor, the head of Paramount, offered to raise her salary to $18,000 a week, but she wanted fifty per

cent of the profits as well. Even he was unable to meet this demand and the association came to an end.

Her new marriage, like most of her unions, was a curious affair. The amiable Marquis had an aristocratic title, but no money, and Swanson was obliged to pay him a salary as a member of her production company. By now she had embarked on an ill-fated path as producer of her own films, with the intention of releasing them through United Artists. Joseph P Kennedy, the formidable millionaire father of a family that would include a charismatic President, an Attorney-General and a Senator, came forward as her financial partner, and arranged for the Marquis to head the Paris office of

RIGHT SWANSON RELAXES AT HOME IN CLUTTERED INFORMALITY. SUCH SHOTS OF STARS' DOMESTICITY WERE MUCH SOUGHT AFTER BY FAN MAGAZINES.

ABOVE GLORIA SWANSON IN 1925, AT THE HEIGHT OF HER FAME, THE TOP BOX-OFFICE STAR OF PARAMOUNT.

Pathé, paving the way for an amicable divorce. Meanwhile Kennedy, the head of a powerful Catholic family, and Swanson pursued an extra-marital affair, incurring the wrath of the church, although steps were taken to hide it from the fans.

Swanson's first independent film, *The Loves of Sunya*, had exceeded its budget and was unfavourably received but her next, *Sadie Thompson*, directed by Raoul Walsh from W Somerset Maugham's novel and play *Rain*, in which she played a prostitute in Pago Pago who is reformed and then raped by a religious fanatic, was a critical and financial success in spite of serious production difficulties including censorship problems.

But Swanson's career fumbled badly when Kennedy signed Erich von Stroheim to direct her in an exotic story created specially for her which was eventually called *Queen Kelly*. Stroheim projected the impression of

having been a Prussian aristocrat and former cavalry officer; in reality he was the son of a Jewish hatter from Silesia, and had briefly served in the Austro-Hungarian army where he had proved to be an accomplished fencer. After working in his father's straw-hat factory, he emigrated to America around 1909, making a living in menial jobs and reached Hollywood in 1914, where he joined D W Griffith as a bit player and assistant director. The entry of America into the First World War enabled him to play a series of coldly sadistic, monocled Hun officers in several films, and he soon became known to audiences as 'The Man You Love To Hate', a designation that caused him when making public appearances to be subjected to abuse and hurled missiles.

Following the Armistice, and the drying-up of such roles, he was able to turn to direction, and wrote and starred in *Blind Husbands*, after having coaxed Carl Laemmle, the founder of Universal, into financing him. A daring tale of a sexual triangle, it was both a commercial and critical success, and also gave Universal artistic cachet as well as healthy box-office returns. But by the time Stroheim made his third film, *Foolish Wives*, signs of hubris were beginning to show, due to problems such as his passion for minor detail. For instance, the extras playing the Austrian guards had to wear the correct and expensively acquired regulation underwear, even though it was never visible. Such needless extravagance was causing consternation in the financial department as the budget soared towards an unprecedented $1 million, according to exaggerated publicity releases trying to make the best out of bad news. Much of the production costs were on the gigantic set of Monte Carlo that sprouted near Lankershim Boulevard. Even though the film turned out be another box-office hit, the final cut had been handed on to others, with a third of Stroheim's footage deleted. He was then fired by Irving Thalberg while making *Merry-Go-Round* and it was completed by Rupert Julian, later the director of Lon Chaney's hugely successful *The Phantom of the Opera*. Stroheim, with extraordinary tenacity, then started his masterpiece, *Greed*, adapted from Frank Norris's novel *McTeague*. Its climax was set in the merciless heat of Death Valley, where conditions for both cast and crew verged on the life-threatening. The finished film was un-releasable, being a staggering forty-two reels long, which would have meant a playing time of more than seven hours. It was whittled down in stages to a mere ten reels, but it still had a striking effect on audiences when eventually released. By now, Stroheim's reputation as a director was tarnished by his extravagant disregard for budgetary constraints, although remarkably he was still able to make *The Merry Widow*, Lehar's light opera, bizarre black comedy, and *The Wedding March*, a study of Hapsburg society, that was so long even in its unfinished state that it was released in Europe as two separate films.

Swanson's apprehensions with regard to *Queen Kelly* were justified, with not only the budget escalating out of control, having doubled with no sign that shooting was nearing an end, but also Stroheim was injecting perverse and erotic touches into the film. He was even reshooting scenes that had already been cleared by the Hays

Office, the body responsible for preserving the industry's moral standards, and was piling up enormous problems for the release. Swanson was forced to fire Stroheim, and then spent another $200,000 trying to cut the mass of footage into shape.

Meanwhile, a revolution was taking over the film industry. It had begun relatively modestly in 1927 when Warner opened an indifferent and schmaltzy musical called *The Jazz Singer*, starring Al Jolson, who had delivered songs with synchronized sound via the Vitaphone disc system. In spite of initial scepticism the silent film era had come to an end. Cinemas all over the world were rapidly

———— ◆ ————

BELOW ERICH VON STROHEIM, A LEGENDARY HOLLYWOOD FIGURE FRESHLY ENCOUNTERING SWANSON AS MAX IN *SUNSET BOULEVARD*.

PICTURE PLAY

DECEMBER 1929

25 cts.

STREET AND SMITH

Gloria Swanson
Painted by
MODEST STEIN

Stingy Stars of Hollywood

LEFT IN THE 1920S AND 1930S SCORES OF FAN MAGAZINES CAPITALIZED ON WORLD-WIDE INTEREST IN THE ACTIVITIES OF THE STARS. SWANSON FREQUENTLY APPEARED ON COVERS.

soon forgotten; an expensive, abandoned failure. It was also the final curtain for Stroheim as a director, although he would make a reasonably successful career in talkies as an actor, with his performance as a wounded aristocrat in a neck-brace, relegated to the running of a prisoner-of-war camp in Jean Renoir's *La Grande Illusion*, among his finest subsequent work.

When the talkies arrived some of the idols of the silent cinema failed to make the transition, although the numbers were actually far fewer than received wisdom would suggest. Those who found they were incapable of the new form of acting, which required under-statement in place of previously exaggerated pantomime gesturing, simply decided that it was time to retire. Others made the sad discovery that their voices failed to record well, particularly on the earliest equipment which seemed to favour a high tonal register, or that their diction was poor and untrained. Many had accents that sounded uncouth on the screen, and Hollywood became a paradise for voice coaches, as well as a target for theatri-cally experienced actors who arrived from Broadway and the West End.

wiring up to play the new talkies, while studios were hastily soundproofing their stages and learning entirely new techniques for making films. Many that were still in pro-duction were given tacked-on reels with added sound, or were stopped and reshot as talkies. The British-born director Edmund Goulding attempted to turn part of *Queen Kelly* into a talking picture, but without suc-cess. Swanson managed to have new footage shot, and a version of the film was given a few screenings in Europe, but remained unseen in the United States, where it was

Norma Talmadge failed the voice test. The prissy articulation of William Haines did not match his tough appearance. The heavily-accented Pola Negri and Greta Nissen quietly faded, the latter to the ignominy of appearing in British quota quickies. There was much apprehension as to how Greta Garbo, the screen's most prominent dramatic actress who had arrived in America from Stockholm in 1925, would adapt to the talking picture. Care was taken to avoid rushing her, and it was not until 1930, when technical standards had greatly improved, that she made her speaking debut in *Anna Christie*. Audiences reacted favourably, in spite of her heavy Swedish accent, as she spoke her deathless first line: 'Gif me a visky, ginger ale on the side, and don't be stingy, baby.' John Gilbert, her romantic partner in several popular hits, was less fortunate. Although he made a total of ten talkies, he was never able to generate the same aura with his voice that he could manage with his silent presence and he died an early, bitter death.

Charlie Chaplin responded to the arrival of talkies by defiantly making *City Lights*, a great silent picture, albeit with a synchronized score. Pickford and Fairbanks turned to Shakespeare with their version of *The Taming of the Shrew*, with the famous credit title 'additional dialogue by Sam Taylor', but both were unhappy with the talkies and eventually dropped out. So did Clara Bow, Colleen Moore and Marion Davies, whose careers were probably due to have ended anyway.

Was Gloria Swanson a victim of the sound revolution? The evidence is that she was not, but she was reaching the natural end of a star's brief life cycle. Her adjustment to the new medium was swift and smooth, and *The Trespasser*, directed by Edmund Goulding shortly after the *Queen Kelly* débâcle, was one of her most successful pictures, earning her an Academy Award nomination. The affair with Kennedy ended abruptly after the box-office failure of *What a Widow!* and after a series of poor choices of subject matter, including *Perfect Understanding*, a film made in England at the newly-opened ATP studios at Ealing, in which her co-star was a young and green Laurence Olivier, she faded quietly from the screen, making her only appearance for several years in a comedy with Adolphe Menjou in 1941 called *Father Takes a Wife*. Her last film before a seven-year hiatus was the unsuccessful screen version of a 1932 Broadway musical *Music in the Air*, by Jerome Kern and Oscar Hammerstein II, the team that had been responsible for the memorable *Showboat*.

Unfortunately, *Music in the Air* had little of the same appeal in spite of its score, and her co-star, John Boles, who had been given his first screen role by her seven years earlier in *The Loves of Sunya*, was wooden. The producer was Erich Pommer, late of UFA in Berlin who, because he was Jewish, had fled from the Nazis and had become a producer at Fox. The director was another German exile, Joe May, who in 1917 had given Fritz Lang his first screenwriting job. May's career was never to flourish in Hollywood, but there was a third Jewish emigré connected with *Music in the Air* who was on the threshold of a glittering career in American cinema. Co-writing the screenplay in collaboration with Howard Young was Billy Wilder, who had reached Hollywood via Paris and Mexico.

Samuel Wilder, nicknamed Billy by his mother, was born in Sucha, Galicia, a hundred miles east of Vienna, on 22 June 1906, the second of two sons. Then Galicia was firmly within the territory of the huge Austro-Hungarian empire; today it is part of Poland. Wilder's father ran a chain of railway station cafés throughout the province; later he opened a hotel in Krakow. In his youth Billy Wilder was obsessed with things American, such as movies, pop songs, dance-steps and cars, and he cultivated a detailed knowledge of all of them. At his mother's behest he enrolled as a law student at the University of Vienna, but quit his course after a mere three months, to become a feature writer on a new magazine. Although the job was poorly paid, it provided him with a great deal of varied experience. On one extraordinary day he interviewed not only Richard Strauss, Arthur Schnitzler and Alfred Adler, but even had an unfruitful encounter with Sigmund Freud. He also developed a talent as a sportswriter.

When in 1926, Paul Whiteman, the self-styled 'King of Jazz', announced that he would be touring Europe with his orchestra, Wilder volunteered his services as an interpreter, and his three-week acquaintance with the band enabled him to expand his already extensive grasp of colloquial American-English. It also took him to Berlin for the first time, and he discovered that the creative juices flowed so powerfully there that he never went back to live in Vienna. Finding that he could pursue a career in the vibrant German capital as a freelance journalist (his first piece was a profile of Whiteman for the *Berliner Zeitung*), he moved in and out of the show business set with ease. Among his friends with whom he was sometimes suspected of having a long-running affair was a small-part actress who would later become a locally prominent film and cabaret star, Marlene Dietrich.

Wilder compensated for occasional shortfalls in income when his journalism work dried up by taking on unusual jobs, such as escorting the visiting American director Allan Dwan and his new wife on conducted tours round Germany, often making up the information he was imparting rather than first consulting the guide book. There were also a number of disreputable ways in which to boost his income. The most notorious, as he himself has described it, was as a gigolo. Wilder worked at the Eden Hotel as a taxi dancer, on call to any unattached, usually middle-aged, female who was prepared to pay him to partner her on the dance floor. He was an accomplished dancer and was attractive to women, giving Charleston lessons to whoever desired them. The money earned was satisfying, but he eventually ruined his lucrative sideline by publishing a series of exposé articles in the *Berliner Zeitung*. A fast and prolific writer, Wilder became intrigued with the possibility of selling stories to films, going to considerable lengths to inveigle introductions to prominent figures in the flourishing industry. They proved effective. In the initial stages he was hired as a ghostwriter, sub-contracted to churn out scripts for established writers who

---

RIGHT BILLY WILDER, THE DIRECTOR OF *SUNSET BOULEVARD*, POSES WITH A PUBLICITY DEPARTMENT PROP UNSEEN IN THE FILM.

did not have sufficient time to meet their own contractual liabilities. Wilder's break came when he worked on *People on Sunday*, an avant-garde feature in a documentary style directed by Robert Siodmak, who would go on to become a prominent filmmaker in Hollywood. There was much talent present on such a modest film. The camera assistant was Fred Zinnemann, who would later direct *High Noon* and become a lifelong friend of Wilder. The cinematographer was Eugen Schüfftan, later Eugene Schuftan, inventor of the Schüfftan process, which combined miniatures with foreground action in one shot. The co-director was Edgar Ulmer, who would become a renowned director of low-budget crime and horror films and a cult figure among French *cinéastes*. In the next four years Wilder scripted about a dozen

films. Some bore his credit and there were many others that did not.

Hitler came to power in January 1933 and Wilder, a Jew, decided that he would have to flee Germany. He went to Paris, where he directed for the first time. The film was *Mauvaise Graine* (*Bad Seed*) and starred the seventeen-year-old Danielle Darrieux. He was now desperately keen to reach America, and sent a screenplay speculatively to Hollywood, addressed to Joe May, his former friend who had become a producer at Columbia. May sent him a one-way ticket and promised him work. Wilder eventually reached Los Angeles circuitously via Mexico and New York, and set to work in the Columbia writers' building, learning English as he went along. When May left Columbia for Fox, Wilder went with him to co-write the

◆

BELOW THE STRIP IN 1950; CHATEAU MARMONT CENTRE RIGHT.

ABOVE THE STRIP AT NIGHT, 1950.
CIRO'S NIGHTCLUB CLOSED IN 1957,
AND IS NOW THE COMEDY STORE.

indifferent *Music in the Air*; Gloria Swanson's attempt to resuscitate her slipping career.

During this period Wilder was suffering from the constant rejection of his scripts, and eking out a bare living. He learned what it was like to be behind on the payments for his car and to be rebuffed by his own agent. His $75 a month room in the Chateau Marmont apartment hotel on Sunset Boulevard was small, with a Murphy bed folded up into a wall cavity by day. The Chateau had opened in 1929 as a modestly-priced apartment hotel when Sunset was still unpaved, but by the 1930s it was part of the landscape of the rapidly developing Strip. This unincorporated stretch of the highway was, until 1984, administered by Los Angeles County. Outside the city's jurisdiction, and so relatively easy

for places of entertainment to operate there, at night the Strip was alive with smart restaurants, bars, cabarets and nightclubs, such as La Boheme, the Ballyhoo, the Vendome, the Club Seville, the Clover Club, the Trocadero, Ciro's, and many others. By day most of the Strip was a tawdry wasteland of garish billboards and temporary-looking buildings, a look that has been perpetuated and given a protected status for the benefit of tourists by the city of West Hollywood of which it now forms part.

Wilder's Hollywood breakthrough came when he was teamed with another writer, the smoothly elegant east coast Anglo-Saxon, Charles Brackett. They were commissioned to write a screenplay for Ernst Lubitsch, the Berlin director Wilder idolized. The picture was

Bluebeard's Eighth Wife, which had been filmed in 1923 by Sam Wood with Gloria Swanson. Their talkie version, starring Gary Cooper and Claudette Colbert, is far superior, in no small part on account of the brisk, bright and sharp Brackett-Wilder dialogue. The new team went on to write a number of other films, including the screwball comedy *Midnight*, again with Colbert in the lead, and *Ninotchka* in which Lubitsch directed Garbo in a comedy, billed as 'Garbo laughs!'. The team also wrote Charles Boyer's film, *Hold Back the Dawn*, and the outstanding Howard Hawks comedy, *Ball of Fire*, starring Gary Cooper and Barbara Stanwyck.

Wilder wanted to direct, mainly because he wished to protect his output, having had bad experiences with certain directors, most notably Mitchell Leisen, who had distorted his work. The opportunity arose with *The Major and the Minor*, in which a hard-up Ginger Rogers was required to pose as a twelve-year-old in order to obtain a cheap rail fare home, and was befriended by a dashing army officer played by Ray Milland, who could not understand why he was so attracted to a pre-teenager. Wilder suspected that the film was not expected to do well, and that the studio was merely humouring him in order to get the directing bug out of his system. It turned out to be a satisfying hit, brilliantly skirting the edge of bad taste with witty insouciance, thus anticipating the tone of some of Wilder's later works such as *Some Like It Hot* and *The Apartment*.

For the rest of the term of his screenwriting association he would direct and Brackett would produce their screenplays. Wilder's next film, again co-scripted with Brackett,

was *Five Graves to Cairo*, an effective reworking of an old play which they turned into a topical comment on the war in the Libyan desert and which was notable for the extraordinary performance of Erich von Stroheim as Field Marshal Rommel. Typically, Stroheim, having learned that the Afrika Korps commander was a dedicated photographer, insisted that the three Leica cameras slung around his neck be loaded with film, although he was never seen to shoot anything with them.

Wilder's next film was without Brackett who demurred, finding the subject too distasteful. Instead, his screenplay collaborator was the great thriller writer Raymond Chandler, who was then unused to the working methods of the Hollywood film industry. The source material was a novel by James M Cain, which Wilder and Chandler transformed into one of the finest of all *films noirs*. The man in *Double Indemnity* enters the dark world of a hugely manipulative, sensual woman who lives in a large old Hollywood house, still standing today at 6301 Quebec Drive. He is weak-willed and is persuaded to become a key part of her plot to murder her rich husband, in order to collect the proceeds of a life policy he has negotiated with her, since he is an insurance salesman. Barbara Stanwyck played Phyllis Dietrichson, the woman, Fred MacMurray was her dupe, and the third main character was played by Edward G Robinson, as MacMurray's shrewd boss and surrogate father-figure who gradually unravels the plot. Daringly, the film opens with the revelation that the crime has gone wrong, and MacMurray is dying. He relates the entire story in flashback.

ABOVE Fred MacMurray and Barbara Stanwyck
in *Double Indemnity*, a *noir* classic
directed in 1944 by Billy Wilder, and scripted
in collaboration with Raymond Chandler.

The central performances are exemplary, particularly that of Stanwyck who had appeared in many gutsy female parts in a career that went back to the beginning of talkies, but had never before been given such a substantial *femme fatale* role. MacMurray, too, hitherto known mainly for 'nice-guy' roles, was also called upon to go against his stereotype. What humour there was in the film occurred in the pithy repartee between the principals, and in the ironies revealed in the plot. The murder, not seen but heard, is all the more brutal for its lack of explicitness and over the whole film hangs a pall of crepuscular evil.

If *Double Indemnity* ratified Wilder's credentials with the critics as well as the public, his next film gained him total respect from the film community. It had, for its time, a daring theme: a hero in an advanced stage of alcoholism, enduring the hallucinatory symptoms of *delirium tremens*. The experience of working with the severely bottle-plagued Chandler was still close to Wilder. Brackett had an intimate knowledge of drunks, too. His wife and daughter both became alcoholics, and his friends had included such talented inebriates as F Scott Fitzgerald, Dorothy Parker and Dashiell Hammett. The film, *The Lost Weekend*, as well as achieving huge box-office success, won Academy Awards for best picture, best actor (Ray Milland), best screenplay (Brackett and Wilder) and best director. Based on a novel by Charles Jackson, it covered a few days in the life of a dipsomaniac writer (Milland) on a serious bender, with bottles hidden all over his New York apartment. Memorable scenes included his trudg-

ing for miles along Third Avenue trying to hock his typewriter at Yom Kippur when all the pawnshops are closed, and a harrowing spell in the alcoholic ward of the Bellevue hospital. The subject was treated with a frankness that was unusual at a time when the Production Code tended to refine gritty realism into an acceptably anodyne form.

At the end of the war Wilder returned to a devastated Germany as a colonel in the US Army's Psychological Warfare Division, charged with the task of salvaging what was left of the German film industry. He drew on his experiences for *A Foreign Affair*, which was an astringent, cynical comedy set against a background of ruined Berlin in which a visiting congressional committee comes up against the black market, and the formidable form of Wilder's friend of later Weimar days, Marlene Dietrich. Some of his detractors found the setting too bleak for the wisecracking script, and accused Wilder, inured to such attacks, of poor taste.

Before he made *A Foreign Affair* he embarked on his first film in Technicolor and a work that seems a bewildering choice for the team responsible for *Double Indemnity* and *The Lost Weekend*. A soft-centred musical set in 1900, *The Emperor Waltz* has Bing Crosby as an American phonograph salesman attempting to interest the Emperor Franz Josef of Austria in his wares and falling for his niece, played by Joan Fontaine. Critics disliked it but the box-office returns satisfied Paramount. It was as though Wilder was exorcizing some atavistic vision of the Austria of his father's youth, and perhaps attempting a homage to the spirit of Ernst Lubitsch, who died while it was being made.

In early 1949 Brackett and Wilder began writing what was to be a seminal film about Hollywood itself, *Sunset Boulevard*. It was their last collaboration, each going their separate ways when the film was finished. Their fourteen-year relationship, while fruitful, had not been without occasional moments of rancour, which was understandable in that the volatile Wilder had little temperament in common with the urbane, sophisticated Brackett. After a fierce quarrel over a montage scene in *Sunset Boulevard*, Wilder vowed that he would never work with Brackett again, and kept his word. After propelling Marilyn Monroe into stardom in *Niagara*, Charles Brackett pursued a successful career as a producer.

Forty-four years on, Billy Wilder, now aged eighty-seven, still spends most of his day working in his office in the Golden Triangle of Beverly Hills, one storey above a gift shop that is just off the expensive shopping street, Rodeo Drive, southern California's own Rue du Faubourg St Honoré. It is an agreeable work-place, crammed with mementoes from his career in cinema that reaches back to 1929. Almost every inch of wallspace is filled with modern paintings and hanging ornaments. The most prominent object, in constant view, is a large round clock, precisely adjusted to the second, that would not look out of place in a bank or the waiting room of a large station. Wilder sits with his back to the window, his visitor in a classic Charles Eames chair, with its accompanying Ottoman close by should it be needed. On the far wall facing Wilder's desk is a framed question, handsomely lettered in a flowing script by Saul Steinberg. It reads: 'How would

Lubitsch do it?' It is as though Wilder needs a constant reminder of his idol to keep his *chutzpah* in control. On a shelf above a collection of Morocco-bound scripts of most of his films, and near a small platoon of seven Oscars is a Prussian spiked helmet; in the corner behind his desk is a multi-coloured old manual typewriter garnished with brilliantly-painted tanks, eagles and the stars and

BELOW BILLY WILDER STAYED AROUND LONG ENOUGH TO BECOME HOLLYWOOD'S GREATEST LIVING DIRECTOR.

ABOVE SWANSON AND WILDER ENJOYED RAPPORT ON *SUNSET BOULEVARD*.

stripes. It has been decorated by Wilder himself, and turned into an artefact which he
calls 'Stallone's Typewriter'. The embellishing
of *objêts* is one of his hobbies. On another
shelf arc a series of heads of Nefertiti, each
with a crown painted in the style of a different artist; a Jackson Pollock Nefertiti, a Piet
Mondrian Nefertiti, a Joan Miro Nefertiti. 'I'm
working on Dali,' says Wilder.

He is wryly amused that as an octoge-
narian he is collecting awards for lifetime
achievement. The European Film Academy
has given him one. In February of 1993 a
special Golden Bear was presented to him at
the Berlin Film Festival. 'As you get older you
can count on getting haemorrhoids and
awards,' he says. They are, he thinks, an
indication that he is not expected to produce
any more work, although he would be very
happy to make another film. Like some other
great Hollywood directors such as Hitchcock,
Huston, Cukor, he does not subscribe too
happily to the notion of retirement. His later
works, including *The Front Page*, *Fedora* and
Buddy, Buddy were box-office disappoint-
ments, and although each of them contains
rewards for his adherents, in the eyes of the
Hollywood shot-callers they cancel out his

prodigiously successful record and he has been fallow since 1981. His creativity is still vibrant, and physically he is like a man fifteen years younger. He is a good talker, but incapable of ever sitting still while he is in flow, preferring to prowl around the room delivering his sharp, witty monologues in an accent that remains heavily Germanic after nearly sixty years of living in America. Wilder mastered the English, or rather, the American language, down to the most obscure slang idioms with such consummate application that he could easily have held a university chair in linguistics. However, he has never managed to lose his accent, even though on occasions he has been embarrassed and angry when it has been mocked.

How did the idea of *Sunset Boulevard* originate? 'I always have a drawer full of little snips of ideas. Perhaps a scene, a character, a line. I said to Brackett one day, "How about an old star who has lost her standing, in the interregnum of silent pictures and sound pictures?"' There was a third screenwriter teamed with Brackett and Wilder on *Sunset Boulevard*. D M Marshman Jr had been a film critic for the weekly magazine, *Life*, and according to Brackett, it was he who first suggested the idea of a relationship between the faded star and a young man.

Their original concept would have produced an entirely different film. Wilder wanted to make an acerbic attack on Hollywood, an outrageous satire on ambition and the part played by sex appeal and in the lead he wanted a screen legend, Mae West, making a comeback. She had not been in a film since 1943, but her ample figure was as voluptuous as it was in her cinematic heyday of *She Done*

Him Wrong, I'm No Angel and *Belle of the Nineties* in the 1930s. Encased in the loving grasp of her powerful corsetry, she had parodied sexual appeal in an unbridled, lusty and entirely idiosyncratic manner, frequently provoking outrage among the censorious. Had she played Norma Desmond, her Joe Gillis would have been devoured.

West, for all Wilder's admiration for her vulgar, earthy view of sex, could not in spite of blandishments be enticed, and the trio gave up pressing her further. Without her, the tone of the idea began to change. Running down the list of great names of the silent cinema whose careers seemed not to have survived the advent of sound, Wilder next sought out Pola Negri, a star for Lubitsch in Germany who had moved on to Hollywood where she had become renowned for her dark, exotic appearance and for an intense affair with Valentino. As his body lay in state in New York she had generated world headlines by swooning over his coffin. Wilder tracked her down to her home in San Antonio and telephoned her. He found her thick Polish accent almost unintelligible, and visualized appalling problems on the set, where his own would have been quite enough of a burden for the crew.

'In another bout of insanity,' said Wilder, explaining the search 'we went up to Pickfair, Mr Brackett and I, to pitch it to Mary Pickford, and halfway through we saw her fallen face was falling some more, as if she was saying "Are they mad? This is me, Mary Pickford, America's darling. I am to play a woman who seduces a writer twenty years younger and gives him presents?" So in the middle of it we stopped and said "Miss

Pickford, we are in grave error. This is certainly not the way we remember you, the way you were at your height. Forgive us," and we backed out of the house.'

It was the director George Cukor who suggested Gloria Swanson to them. For some unremembered reason Wilder and Brackett had omitted her from their considerations, in spite of the fact that she had been the greatest star on the Paramount lot, their own studio. It was as if subconsciously they had excluded her because she was beyond attainment. She had long quit the screen and was living in New York. In her memoirs, *Swanson on Swanson*, she describes how, having been out of the film world for so many years, she was astonished to receive Wilder's call and had to check with her friend, Cukor, that it was the right thing to go to California for a meeting with them. Cukor assured her that Brackett and Wilder were the hottest young team working in Hollywood. So she made the journey. Wilder, who had only a brief recollection

◆

BELOW THE *SUNSET BOULEVARD* PRINCIPALS: WILLIAM HOLDEN, GLORIA SWANSON, NANCY OLSON AND ERICH VON STROHEIM. NEITHER HOLDEN NOR SWANSON WERE WILDER AND BRACKETT'S FIRST CHOICES.

ABOVE SUNSET'S 10000-BLOCK IN 1949, THE DESMOND MANSION SITE.

of her in the forgettable *Music in the Air*, was immediately impressed with her profile.

'Remember her line: "They had faces then"? Well, she had a face that could not be duplicated. That goes for Bardot, Dietrich and Marilyn Monroe. Swanson was small, but perfect. She knew how to act with gestures, something difficult to teach. Now we began to have great luck. We needed DeMille, we got DeMille. We needed Stroheim, we got Stroheim. We needed Stroheim to project a picture that he had directed and we got *Queen Kelly*, done with the money of Papa Kennedy, by the way. With Swanson. We needed a bridge party of old stars and we got Buster Keaton, H B Warner who had played Jesus in *King of Kings*, and Anna Q Nilsson. You could not do much better. We got every conceivable lucky break you can think of.'

Not entirely. There were problems over the leading man. Montgomery Clift, who had won an Academy Award for his first film, *The Search*, directed by Fred Zinnemann, and was then completing *The Heiress* at

Paramount for William Wyler, had agreed to play the young writer. Then two weeks before the start of shooting, he withdrew, possibly on the advice of his agent who was unhappy at him playing the love object of a much older woman. There was a reason. Clift had a liaison, unknown to the public, with Libby Holman, a popular torch singer of the 1920s, whose career had collapsed following a scandal in which her husband had been shot by her, although it was judged to have been an accident. She had become an alcoholic, and part of Clift's shadowy background; he spent much of his time living in her New England mansion. For him to have played Joe Gillis would have set the press prying into his world.

With two weeks to go, the list of Paramount contract actors was carefully scanned. William Holden had been in films for a decade, attaining stardom in 1939 as the young boxer in *Golden Boy*, directed by Rouben Mamoulian from the Clifford Odets play. His subsequent films had been unremarkable, and he generally played clean-cut, short-haircut, 'smiling Jims'. When he was approached for *Sunset Boulevard* he was thirty-one, which made him slightly too old to play Joe Gillis, and Swanson was initially apprehensive that the gap between them was not pronounced enough. She was at that time fifty-one, roughly the age Norma Desmond was supposed to be in the script. Wilder assured her that he would be given 'young' make-up, which turned out to mean little, since the screenplay made it clear that the character had spent several years working on an Ohio newspaper, followed by three years in California, and so would have been in his late twenties at very least.

Apart from Erich von Stroheim as Max, the star's devoted retainer, and the young actress needed to play Betty Schaefer, the only other major casting was that of Norma Desmond's mansion, which was meant to be located in the 10000 block of Sunset Boulevard in the Holmby Hills. In reality the chosen house, which had to be opulent, overpowering, architecturally passé, with neglected grounds, was several miles away at 3810 Wilshire Boulevard, on the corner of Crenshaw and Irving. It had been built in 1924 for William Jenkins on a two-acre site, and eventually became part of the divorce settlement of the second Mrs J Paul Getty. The only major amendment to its exterior, apart from the addition of foliage, was the installation of a swimming pool which looked convincing, but lacked any means of circulating its water, and so was useless when filming had finished, although the owner was content. In its empty condition it did make one further screen appearance, in Nicholas Ray's 1955 film with James Dean, *Rebel Without a Cause*. Two years later the house was demolished, and a dull, twenty-two storey office building for Getty Oil was erected and still stands on the site.

There are many points of similarity between *Sunset Boulevard* and Wilder's film of six years earlier, *Double Indemnity*. Joe Gillis, like Walter Neff, encounters a lone woman in a stuffy, mausoleum-like Hollywood mansion, and allows himself to become the instrument for enacting her egocentric purpose. Both stories are told in flashback, and audiences are aware at the start that whatever went on turned into disaster. Neff is a dying man delivering his account to an office dictating machine in the small hours of the morning. Joe Gillis manages to go even better; he is already dead, and he comments on the recovery of his body from the swimming pool with a number of bullet holes in it. Both films have a blameless, unsullied figure who hears the confession. In the former case it is Edward G Robinson as Barton Keyes, Neff's admirable boss, and in the latter, Betty Schaefer, to whom both Norma and Joe reveal their living arrangements at the dramatic climax. Each film is in the *noir*-style, with the characteristic deep, nocturnal shadows, expressionistic lighting, off-screen narration in flashback, and above all, a weak hero destroyed by a manipulative woman in a tragic, romantic liaison. It is as if Wilder had decided to use a similar framework on which to hang a baroque elaboration, substituting Norma Desmond's blind ambition for Phyllis Dietrichson's profane avarice.

In the brilliant opening sequence, after the film's title is seen stencilled on a kerb (abbreviated as Sunset Blvd, which as far as the Library of Congress is concerned is the correct title, since the rule is that a film's credits are considered definitive) the camera pulls back to reveal a cortège of wailing police vehicles sweeping along the tree-lined boulevard just after first light and turning off into a driveway. Policemen swarm towards the swimming pool where a body is floating, face down. A stunning shot follows, with the camera apparently looking up from the bottom of the pool at the dead man's face, and behind him the police officers on the poolside. Technically it was a difficult shot to make because it is not possible to shoot through water and get a clear image beyond. Wilder and his director of photography, John Seitz, solved the problem by fixing a large mirror on the bottom of the pool and focusing into its reflection. The floating man is William Holden, who begins his voice-over; one of the few instances in which a narration has been supplied by a dead person. It is not the original opening, and was shot long after the completion of principal photography.

———————— ◆ ————————

BELOW THE CORPSE OF JOE GILLIS IS FISHED FROM THE POOL AT THE START OF *SUNSET BOULEVARD*.

A HOLLYWOOD STORY

Sensational...
Daring...
Unforgettable!

SUNSET BOULEVARD

WILLIAM **HOLDEN** · GLORIA **SWANSON** · ERICH von **STROHEIM**

STARRING NANCY OLSON · FRED CLARK · LLOYD GOUGH · JACK WEBB

AND CECIL B. DeMILLE · HEDDA HOPPER · BUSTER KEATON · ANNA Q. NILSSON · H.B. WARNER · FRANKLYN FARNUM Jr

PRODUCED BY CHARLES BRACKETT · DIRECTED BY BILLY WILDER · WRITTEN BY CHARLES BRACKETT, BILLY WILDER AND D.M. MARSHMAN Jr

A PARAMOUNT PICTURE

DISTRIBUTED BY PARAMOUNT FILM SERVICE LTD.

LEFT BRITISH POSTER FOR *SUNSET*.
SHOULD IT BE *BOULEVARD* OR *BLVD*?

'The picture started originally,' said Wilder, 'with a hearse delivering a corpse to the LA morgue, where it's brought to join six or eight other corpses, covered in sheets, and then the corpses tell each other the events leading to their death. When it reaches Holden the story starts.' The sequence was actually shot. According to the screenplay, an attendant ties a linen tag to the left big toe of the new arrival on which is stated: JOSEPH GILLIS, HOMICIDE, 5/17/49. The corpse is then moved into a bleak, windowless room to join the others. After the attendant has gone the corpses begin to talk, like schoolboys in a dorm after lights-out. A fat man declares he died of a heart attack, a small boy held his breath too long underwater, a black truck-driver was killed by a woman in a Chevrolet coupé and is anxious to know if the White Sox were beaten in their game that followed his death.

FAT MAN: *Where did you drown? The ocean?*

GILLIS: *No. Swimming pool.*

FAT MAN: *A husky fellow like you?*

GILLIS: *Well, I had a few extra holes in me. Two in the chest, and one in the stomach.*

FAT MAN: *You were murdered?*

GILLIS: *Yes, I was murdered.*

It is fortunate that a decision was taken to preview the finished film in order to gauge audience reaction, a common precaution for the bigger pictures, usually with the intention of determining the appropriate marketing approach. There was some apprehension at Paramount that the story was too parochial to appeal beyond the industry itself.

'We didn't want to preview the picture in Hollywood,' said Wilder. 'We wanted to take it well away from where they would know the place, so we took it to Evanston, Illinois, just outside Chicago. We previewed it, the picture started and when the tag was looped over the big toe some people started screaming with laughter. You see, people with a new film don't know what to expect, they don't know how to react. It was a terrible night. I had to leave the theatre. I got sick to my stomach and I was sitting on the steps leading to the restrooms, in despair. I looked up and there was a lady coming from the theatre, over-dressed, and she sees me sitting there and she says "Have you ever seen shit like this in your life before?" I said: "Absolutely never. Never." So we previewed it again in Great Neck, New York. The same reaction. So on the way back to Hollywood I said that we were going to have to cut out the morgue scene. It had taken a week to shoot, but I threw it away. I did the same with the ending of *Double Indemnity* where I had MacMurray in the gas chamber. That too cost money.'

In order to shoot the new opening sequence the release of *Sunset Boulevard* was delayed. It is conceivable that the morgue opening would have worked had it prefaced the earlier concept of a satirical film which would have starred Mae West.

Principal photography for *Sunset Boulevard* took place between 11 April and 18 June 1949. The film had been prepared virtually in secret as Wilder was anxious that word should not get around that he was planning an exposé of Hollywood. Its early title, *A Can of Beans*, which there was no intention of ever using on the finished film, was deliberately chosen to be misleading in order to offer no clues with regard to the subject matter. An early draft of the script bore the warning:

THIS IS THE FIRST ACT OF SUNSET BOULEVARD. DUE TO THE PECULIAR NATURE OF THE PROJECT, WE ASK ALL OUR CO-WORKERS TO REGARD IT AS TOP SECRET.
BRACKETT & WILDER

They had a habit of beginning the shooting of their films without a final draft being complete, as much a way of frustrating external attempts to interfere with their work as expediency because they had still not worked out all the details. Notes on drafts indicate substantial revisions, particularly with regard to the names of the characters. Initially the hero was 'Dan Gillis', then he became 'Dick Gillis', the final 'Joe Gillis' being determined almost as the cameras rolled. One of the early memos on casting describes the smaller parts as 'movie people, cops and corpses'. The producer seen in an early scene was originally called Kaufman, and was to be played by Joseph Calleia, who was usually cast as gangsters or other villains. The character name was changed to Millman, and then finally to Sheldrake, with the reliable, bald character actor Fred Clark in the part, providing some of the more overtly humorous moments in *Sunset Boulevard*. Years later, the Fred MacMurray character in *The Apartment* would also be called Sheldrake.

Another production memo requesting changes asks for the Desmond house to be enormous, musty and sombre but to have no tattered hangings. Her car should not be a Rolls-Royce, but a Hispano-Suiza (eventually it was an Isotta-Fraschini). Her writing project should not be her memoirs, but a script for her own version, built around her, of *Salome*. The room over the garage in which Gillis spends his first nights on Norma Desmond's property is not storage space, but the chauffeur's quarters.

The storyline of the finished film is a remarkably adroit, flowing narrative, without the flat spots that can be expected in a 110-minute film. The major part is told in flashback, with a brief epilogue. The posthumous account delivered by Joe Gillis does not reflect great credit on him. He reports, while his floating body is shown on the screen, that he was a failed screenwriter, three months behind on his rent, and anxious to keep his car away from the repossessors. The flashback begins with a view of the Alta-Nido apartments on Franklin and Ivar, a low-rent dwelling house in central Hollywood. The Spanish-style building is still there, maintained in excellent condition and popular

BELOW JOE GILLIS AT WORK ON HIS FOLD-DOWN MURPHY BED IN HIS ONE ROOM ALTA-NIDO APARTMENT.

with a young, upwardly mobile clientele, grateful to reside there during a transient period of their careers.

The finance company men give Joe a twenty-four hour ultimatum, and he has to raise $300 rapidly. He tries to generate interest in a screenplay of a baseball film, *Bases Loaded*, that has been languishing with a producer, Sheldrake. A young script reader, called Betty Schaefer, pours cold water on it, and is then embarrassed to discover that its author is in the room. Joe tries to raise money from his agent, interrupting his golf at the Bel-Air Country Club and succeeds only in antagonizing him. On his way back from Bel-Air, he is bleakly contemplating a return with his tail between his legs to his old job on a newspaper in Dayton, Ohio when he is spotted by the finance men after his car. During a

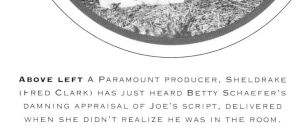

ABOVE LEFT A PARAMOUNT PRODUCER, SHELDRAKE (FRED CLARK) HAS JUST HEARD BETTY SCHAEFER'S DAMNING APPRAISAL OF JOE'S SCRIPT, DELIVERED WHEN SHE DIDN'T REALIZE HE WAS IN THE ROOM.

ABOVE A MONKEY'S FUNERAL: NORMA DESMOND WATCHES MAX INTER HER DECEASED PET, A NOCTURNAL RITE OBSERVED BY JOE FROM THE WINDOW OF HIS BEDROOM OVER THE GARAGE.

ABOVE JOE GILLIS FITS
INTO THE DEMEANING ROLE
OF NORMA DESMOND'S KEPT MAN.

LEFT THE SWIMMING POOL SPECIALLY INSTALLED
AT THE MANSION ON WILSHIRE BOULEVARD USED
FOR EXTERIORS WAS A HOLLYWOOD FAKE – IT HAD
NO PLUMBING AND WAS CONSEQUENTLY UNUSABLE.

chase along a twisting stretch of Sunset
Boulevard he has a blow out, and turns off
the highway into a private driveway. Leaving
his car in a huge garage, deserted except for a
mothballed late-1920s limousine, a hand-
built Isotta-Fraschini, he is spotted by a
woman from the upstairs window of the large
adjacent mansion. She believes that he has
come to inter her deceased pet chimpanzee.
When the confusion is settled he recognizes
her as Norma Desmond, queen of the silent
movies. She is about to dismiss him, but on
learning that he is a writer insists that he read
the monumental script of *Salome* that she
has written and with which she hopes to
make a return to the screen. Sensing a chance
of financial reward, he complies over a period

of several hours, and makes an insincere
judgement on the script's merits, whereupon
he finds himself invited to stay on and put it
into shape. The stiffly formal German butler,
Max, the only other inhabitant of the vast,
gloomy house, shows him to quarters over the
garage. By morning all his possessions are
with him, having been brought from the
apartment by Max who has also paid off the
rent arrears.

In the next weeks, Joe makes the most of
his situation, spinning out the work on the
script by day and watching Norma
Desmond's own films in her presence in the
evenings. The only occasional visitors are
three of her contemporaries who make up
bridge pairs. The repossession men find Joe's

car and tow it away, but then Max restores the Isotta to life. He acts as chauffeur, taking Norma and Joe out. Joe has become a kept man. Norma takes Joe to a menswear shop to be togged out, while a slimy store clerk makes innuendo remarks on his kept-man position. Norma confesses that she loves Joe, and stages an elaborate New Year's Eve party with sumptuous catering and an orchestra, but he discovers that he is the only guest. Unable to take any more, he leaves the house to seek people of his own age, calling on his friend Artie, an assistant director, who is having a crowded New Year party in his apartment. Artie is bemused by Joe's appearance in white tie and tails, and introduces him to Betty, his fiancée, who turns out to be the

girl who had condemned his baseball script in Sheldrake's office. They talk about another of his scripts, which she has read and thinks shows promise. She offers to help in redrafting it. Joe asks Artie if he can move in temporarily and telephones Norma to say he is leaving her, only to learn from Max that she has attempted suicide. Abruptly he exits, rushing back to the Desmond house.

Norma recovers, but now has him under her control. The Salome script is finished and delivered by Max to Cecil B DeMille at Paramount. On an evening excursion Joe steps out of the Isotta at Schwab's drugstore to buy Norma cigarettes and he runs into Betty, who has been trying to find him. She reiterates her wish to collaborate on his

ABOVE THE GRIM NEW YEAR'S PARTY À DEUX. SWANSON LOANED HER OWN SILENT-ERA PORTRAITS.

◆

LEFT SWANSON ON THE NORMA DESMOND TANGO FLOOR, TILED IN ACCORDANCE WITH VALENTINO'S WHIM.

ABOVE NORMA EVOKES JOE'S CONCERN AFTER HER SUICIDE ATTEMPT.

script. He is intrigued but unable to stay talking to her. A few days later a call comes from
Paramount and Norma believes it is from an
emissary of DeMille. She decides to go and
see the director of her greatest triumphs and
is admitted to the lot by an old studio policeman who rebukes his younger colleague for
not recognizing her. DeMille interrupts the
filming of *Samson and Delilah* to greet her
and she drinks in the exultation of being surrounded by those on his set who remember
her. DeMille is tactful and non-committal.
Meanwhile Joe has found Betty's office. She
tells him that Artie is away on location and
that she is willing to work with him on his

script. They are interrupted by Max, who quietly tells Joe that the call from Paramount
was not because the studio wanted Norma
Desmond, but instead her antique car for use
as a prop in a Bing Crosby picture.

It is impossible to tell her the truth.
Convinced that she is to make her return, she
embarks on getting herself in shape with
beauticians, masseuses and dieticians directing her regimen. Joe sneaks out every night to
work with Betty on the deserted Paramount
lot. They fall in love. One night she notices an
intimate message from Norma inside his
expensive cigarette case. Joe dismisses it
lightly. The same night when he returns he

ABOVE PREPARATIONS FOR A RETURN TO THE MOVIES:
NORMA EMBARKS ON A FRENZIED SCHEDULE OF BEAUTY TREATMENTS IN ORDER
TO BE WORTHY OF DEMILLE'S CAMERAS, SO SHE BELIEVES.

finds Max waiting for him in the garage. Max warns that Norma is aware of his nocturnal excursions. He reveals that he was the director of her early films and her first husband, and cannot allow her to be hurt.

Betty, who is on the point of throwing over Artie, gets a call from Norma who has found her number. She begins to hear the dreadful truth of Joe's involvement. Joe walks into Norma's bedroom while she is talking, takes the phone and tells Betty to come to the house. The girl rushes to 10086 Sunset Boulevard. Joe shows her what the old star's mansion looks like and explains his situation, then orders her to go back to Artie. She departs tearfully. He then goes upstairs and begins packing, taking care to leave the clothes and jewellery Norma has bought him. She begs him to stay. Joe starts on his way down the stairs and out of the house. She shoots him, three times, he falls into the

swimming pool and the flashback ends where the film begins, with his body floating face down, observed by the police.

Upstairs Norma, her bedroom thronged with people, has lost her mind. Max agrees with the police to subscribe to the illusion that she is making her new movie in order to get her downstairs and out of the house. The newsreel lights on the staircase convince Norma that her scene is about to be shot. Max calls for action, and she glides down the stairs as the cameras roll, making a speech as she reaches the foot describing how happy she is to be back with her public. She concludes by informing Max, who she now believes is DeMille, that she is ready for her close-up shot.

LEFT THE DESPERATE NORMA DESMOND CROSSES THE BRINK INTO INSANITY AS JOE GILLIS PACKS HIS BAGS. 'NOBODY WALKS OUT ON A STAR', SHE CRIES.

———— ◆ ————

ABOVE THE DRAMATIC CLIMAX OF *SUNSET BOULEVARD*. NORMA SHOOTS JOE DOWN AS HE WALKS OUT ON HER.

———— ◆ ————

RIGHT LETHALLY WOUNDED BY THREE GUNSHOTS, JOE'S CORPSE TOPPLES INTO NORMA'S POOL. 'I ALWAYS WANTED A POOL'.

Gloria Swanson gives a near-perfect rendering of her screen character, with every movement, every vocal inflection precisely calculated. It was a revelation that a great silent-screen actress could speak her lines so appropriately. Wilder found no need to bring down her performance; through intense self-discipline she always remained perfectly in control. 'Nobody could teach that style of acting,' said Wilder, 'you would have had to live it.'

Just under five feet in height (Mary Pickford was even shorter), on screen Swanson seemed to grow in stature. Her interpretation demonstrated a high degree of understanding of the part. Her Norma Desmond is a great star, and can never allow herself to forget it. When Joe eventually walks out on her, she cries: 'No one leaves a star. That's what makes a star.' She is constantly conscious of the necessity, the duty, to give satisfaction to her public which she believes has never deserted her, unaware that most of the fan letters still received each week have been penned by the faithful Max.

Swanson gave an indelible power to such lines as: 'I *am* big. It is the pictures that got small', and an extraordinary moment when she stands in the beam of the projector showing an old film of hers and turns, displaying

ABOVE THE CRAZED NORMA BELIEVES SHE IS AT LAST PLAYING SALOME AS SHE GLIDES DOWN HER STAIRCASE.

her proud, magnificent profile: 'Still wonderful, isn't it? And no dialogue. We didn't need dialogue. We had *faces*. There just aren't any faces like that any more. . .'

There were, as commentators of the time eagerly pointed out, many parallels between Desmond and Swanson. When Desmond tells the policeman on the gate: 'Without me there wouldn't be any Paramount Studios', she speaks words that could equally apply to Swanson, their top star six years running in the 1920s. Swanson also had made many of her most successful films with Cecil B DeMille, who often addressed her as 'young fellow', as he does Norma Desmond. To the younger generation of filmgoers in 1950 Swanson's name would have meant very little, as she had retired more than fifteen years earlier and in the interim had only been on the screen once, in the forgettable *Father Takes a Wife* in 1941.

Conversely, unlike Desmond, Swanson was not a Sunset Boulevard recluse. She had chosen to leave Hollywood on her own terms and embark on a fulfilled life as a successful businesswoman. She was mentally undisturbed and certainly did not have her own 900-page screenplay awaiting the attentions of a producer. On occasions she had been interested in making a return to the screen: in 1937 for instance, she was in talks with Columbia regarding a screenplay about a dying woman, based on a successful Broadway play, that the legendary producer David O Selznick, who had an option, was willing to sell. Harry Cohn, the unattractive tsar of Columbia, then abruptly vetoed the project on the grounds, logical to him, that if Selznick was willing to relinquish it then it

had to be no good. It passed instead to Warner who turned it into one of Bette Davis's most successful films, *Dark Victory*.

Prior to the release of *Sunset Boulevard*, Swanson had been happy to take part in a national tour for Paramount to promote *The Heiress*, which starred Ralph Richardson, Olivia de Havilland and Montgomery Clift, then due to play the Joe Gillis role. Hollywood was at the time suffering bad publicity from various scandals, the most

BELOW CECIL B DeMILLE, CROSSING HER PALM WITH SILVER, IS REUNITED WITH HIS OLD STAR GLORIA SWANSON.

ABOVE AT TWENTY-THREE SWANSON LIVED TO THE HILT AS A SUPERSTAR.

notorious of which was the decamping of the married Ingrid Bergman to join her lover, the Italian director Roberto Rossellini in Europe, and giving birth at a time when illegitimacy attracted moral opprobrium. The machinations of the House Un-American Activities Committee (HUAC) had sapped morale throughout the industry; their unsubtle witch-hunts against suspected communists driving a wedge through the film community, abruptly terminating the careers of those who failed to meet with its approval.

Wilder, a natural subversive, had managed to avoid their attentions. He was careful not to get into an argument with the ultra right-wing Cecil B DeMille, whose role in the hearings had been less than honourable. Wilder, while detesting his politics, admired

DeMille on a professional level, and was willing to acknowledge the extraordinary contribution his epic spectacles had made to the cinema, with their astounding decor, expensive costumes and extravagant story-telling.

In his heyday DeMille, the son of a devout churchman, had been able to brush frontiers of taste aside by depicting lascivious orgies in the context of moralistic biblical works. He was an opportunist, certainly a hypocrite, a great showman and a brilliantly innovative filmmaker who had been a prime mover in establishing Hollywood as the world's film capital. His role as himself in *Sunset Boulevard* was apposite, and he acted the part with conviction, allowing the interruption by Wilder of his current epic, *Samson and Delilah*, which starred Victor Mature and

Hedy Lamarr (apparently not on call on the day Norma Desmond visits his set). No doubt DeMille, always acutely alert to the value of publicity, saw it as a promotional extra for his film which, as it transpired, was released in the year before *Sunset Boulevard*. He is seen, in his customary directing garb of riding breeches and highly-polished boots, in a benign mood, greeting Norma with a genuine paternalistic affection, and tactfully deflecting her remarks about working together again with considerable kindness.

What was it like for Wilder to direct DeMille? 'I had an agreement with him,' said Wilder. 'I would not tell him how to direct *Samson and Delilah*. He would not tell me how to direct *Sunset Boulevard*. He was very professional. I told him what I wanted him to do, he said fine, and asked for a fee of $10,000 which I agreed. Later I had to go back to him to ask for an additional close-up. He said absolutely. That would be another $10,000.'

Wilder, whose reputation for tactlessness had caused him to be barred from more than one dinner table was wary of DeMille. The old director extended a special invitation to Wilder to attend a private screening of the interminable epic that came after *Samson and Delilah*. When the lights went up the moment came when his opinion was sought. 'Cecil,' said Wilder, 'you have made the greatest show on earth.' DeMille beamed with satisfaction. 'Thank you so much, Billy.' Wilder had in fact merely stated the title of the film.

DeMille was not the only major director acting in *Sunset Boulevard*. The other was Wilder's fellow Austrian, Erich von Stroheim,

in the pivotal role of Max von Mayerling, the factotum of the Desmond residence and sometime husband and director. Stroheim had earlier worked with Wilder on *Five Graves to Cairo* giving an excellent performance as Rommel; the part in *Sunset Boulevard* was written for him. 'When he was in a scene you only had to look at the back of his neck, there was something absolutely explosive about that neck,' said Wilder.

Unlike the reticent DeMille, Stroheim was ceaseless with suggestions on how to embellish his character. He asked Wilder to shoot him washing Norma's fragile lingerie, perhaps holding a pair of silken panties to his cheek. Wilder adamantly refused to portray Max as a fetishist. Stroheim asked to be allowed to limp with a clomping gait reminiscent of Boris Karloff in *Frankenstein*. 'You couldn't sit for two hours watching that,' says Wilder, 'I had to talk him out of things. On the other hand I had to listen very carefully because sometimes pearls would come out.'

At the time of filming in 1949 Stroheim told journalist Ezra Goodman: 'I work well with Billy Wilder. He takes suggestions. Some directors I have worked with in the past do not take suggestions from a director of thirty years ago. It's heartbreaking. I just suffer in silence. What is it like to take direction from someone else? Let me put it this way: in order to be a good general, you have to be a good private. In order to be able to give orders, you have to be able to take orders.'

Stroheim was unable to drive, which put him at a disadvantage when he was chauffeuring Norma Desmond's Isotta-Fraschini. The vivid scene in which she is driven up to the old arched Paramount gate on Marathon

Street and has her altercation with a young, inexperienced studio policeman before being rescued by the veteran 'Jonesey', was responsible for several headaches. The car was moved forward by several men pulling on an off-camera rope, while Stroheim gripped the wheel in an unusually intense fury of concentration. 'He still managed to hit the gate,' said Wilder, 'he had no co-ordination.'

Max is a perplexing, almost mystical character. The extent of his duties seem superhuman. There are no other servants in the household, yet it gives the appearance of being properly dusted and tidied, in spite of the heavy, old-fashioned and fussy decor that meets the ideal of what a silent megastar's home should look like. Only the garden and the swimming pool are neglected, and after Joe's arrival even they are miraculously given attention and brought back into use. Max prepares the food, makes the beds, looks after the accounts, runs the projector and plays Bach on the organ (in white gloves, a Stroheim touch). He also finds time to fake the fan letters and to organize a funeral for a simian pet. He whisks Joe's luggage into his bedroom while he is asleep, having picked it up from his apartment and paid off the arrears, but there is no indication how he did it, since the only car on the Desmond premises is at that time out of circulation. Max is at all times tactful, compliant, protective and loyal to his self-absorbed, narcissistic mistress, regarding his role as her buffer from the outside world. It is he who has removed all the door-locks inside the house, and sees to it that there are no sleeping pills or razor blades and that the gas in her bedroom is shut off.

Towards the end of the film, the revelation that Max von Mayerling was the director who made her a star, and also her first husband who then had to see his two successors move into the marital bed, is a shock, but half-suspected. He knows every vain, intimate detail of her and even when she has finally gone insane, it is he who gently allows her to enjoy the last moments of illusion by pretending to be DeMille. Because Stroheim is so mesmeric, understanding and deeply sympathetic in the role, the implausibilities

◆

BELOW BILLY WILDER ADJUSTS A BOOM MICROPHONE, AN EXERCISE EYED BY GLORIA SWANSON WITH APPREHENSIVE DISTASTE.

are not immediately apparent. His casting turned out to be as crucial as that of Swanson in making the film work so well.

Gloria Swanson's last dealings with Stroheim had culminated in her dismissing him over the fiasco of *Queen Kelly*. She was magnanimous, having patched up her professional quarrels with him years earlier, and there was no rancour on the set between them. The film that Swanson watches in the 'they had faces' scene is in fact, *Queen Kelly*, a beautifully lit close-up that exhibited to a generation of filmgoers that had never seen a silent movie the subtle mastery of light and shade achieved then. Wilder had previously screened the European release print of it to Swanson and Stroheim, and they had agreed in her words 'it had weathered the years well, and glowed like a classic.'

Swanson in one of the rare charming moments in *Sunset Boulevard* demonstrated Norma Desmond's fine talent for mimicry by first posing as a Mack Sennett Bathing Beauty with a twirling parasol, and then performing a remarkably accurate impersonation of Charlie Chaplin as the Little Tramp. When the scene was completed she discovered that every member of the cast and crew was suddenly sporting a Chaplin bowler hat.

William Holden, hustled into the role of Joe at the last minute, proved also to be a felicitous choice. Born in Illinois in 1918, and raised in California, he had become an actor

straight from Pasadena Junior College, having been noticed by a Paramount talent scout in a play. He made three more appearances in Wilder films, winning an Academy Award for his part in *Stalag 17*, a 1953 release. At the time of *Sunset Boulevard* he was a screen actor with a decade of experience, but who had still made very little impact, having played mostly bland roles that never caught the imagination of the public. His performance opposite Swanson turned out to be a watershed in his career. As the 1950s progressed he was consistently a top box-office draw.

The hopes that had propelled his character of Joe Gillis from his niche on the rewrite desk of a Dayton evening paper had evaporated in three years of California. Gillis's talent as a screenwriter is a minor one, and whatever integrity he may have started with ('The last one I wrote was about Okies in the Dust Bowl. When they finished with it the whole thing played on a torpedo boat.') has been ironed out of him. For all those who make it in Hollywood ten times as many do not; every waitress seems to be waiting for a studio to call, every hotel clerk has a project 'in development'. Joe Gillis is clinging on by his teeth, he has to hide

———————— ◆ ————————

LEFT A GLIMPSE OF SWANSON'S COMIC TALENT IS REVEALED WHEN AS NORMA SHE IMPERSONATES CHAPLIN FOR JOE'S BENEFIT. THE COMEDIAN ONCE REJECTED HER FOR BEING UNFUNNY.

ABOVE CAST AND CREW PUT ON THEIR CHAPLIN BOWLERS.

his car because he has skipped the payments, he is three months behind on the rent on his apartment, and he has run out of credit with his so-called friends ('I talked to a couple of yes men at Twentieth. To me they said no.').

In spite of his relative youth Joe is already being supplanted by a new generation of filmmakers and audiences. He still advocates social-issue stories which by the beginning of the 1950s had abruptly become an endangered species. A side-effect of the HUAC hearings had been to scare the studios away from subjects that could in any way be interpreted as having a left-wing slant. Out with Dust Bowl Okies, in with Martin and Lewis. Unease hung in the air over Hollywood. Federal legislation following a Supreme Court decision in 1948 had also forced the studios to divest themselves of their exhibition interests, which in Paramount's case were particularly strong in New England and the South. The majors had controlled some seventy per cent of the first-run houses in those American cities with a population over 100,000, and through vertical integration, the means of production, distribution and exhibition, were able to determine the trading conditions, freezing out competitors who did not belong to their club. No longer.

S U N S E T   A N D   A F T E R

ABOVE PARAMOUNT IN 1949, YEAR OF *SUNSET BOULEVARD* AND *SAMSON AND DELILAH*. BEHIND IS THE HOLLYWOOD CEMETERY.

The other scare concerned television, which in 1950 was still a relatively young medium, but growing rapidly. Pessimistic forecasters believed that within a few years it would kill the film business completely. American movie audiences had already declined by a third from their 1945 peak, and would continue to tumble until the 1970s when an upturn began.

One of the casualties of change, gone by the end of the decade, would be the B-feature, the bottom part of the double bill, where the character of Joe Gillis would have achieved his only screen credits. Without knowing it, he has become an anachronism himself, having not adjusted to new conditions. There is no excusable reason for him to be patronizing towards Norma Desmond who had at least achieved great success before finding herself in that state. What is clear from his chance meeting is that he holds her in little respect, having no regard for the heritage of cinema that she represents. 'You used to be big,' he tactlessly observes. Silent cinema is a *passé* world as far as he is concerned, and he describes her contemporary partners at her bridge night, even though they include the great Buster Keaton, as 'waxworks'. He does not acknowledge her stature, and sneers at her old films as though there is something freakish about them, although they were then only just over twenty years old. In fairness, his was a prevailing attitude two decades after the talking picture was introduced. Arthouses and cinematheques were almost unknown, television was barely established, and silent films were simply not shown, known only as titles referred to by those old enough to remember. The wisdom of Gillis's generation was that they were naive, exaggerated, extravagant and comically dated. A side-effect of Wilder's film is that it acts as a corrective to that idea.

Gillis is ready enough to take advantage of his hostess, while only half-aware that she is using him. He resents the advice of the sales clerk in a men's shop to choose the vicuna rather than the camel-hair coat because the lady is paying, but nevertheless follows it. After she has attempted suicide with the razor from his room after his walk out on her elaborate New Year's Eve party *à deux*, he allows himself to be drawn into her bed, quelling feelings of self-loathing by dreaming of Betty Schaefer. Only when Desmond, her madness painfully apparent, has brought Schaefer into the disagreeable situation, does he decide to leave, but he is too insensitive to appreciate the effects of his actions. His disgust with himself is such that before leaving Norma Desmond he relinquishes the clothes and trinkets she has lavished on him, and so shows that he has never really learned the ways of Hollywood; in spirit he is still a provincial newspaper hack.

What of Betty Schaefer, who might have been his salvation? She is played by Nancy Olson, then a young actress of twenty-one, approximately the age of her character. Olson was a college graduate with two other credits including *Union Station* which saw her cast again with William Holden. It was started

ABOVE SWANSON WITH THE WAXWORKS: KEATON, NILSSON AND H B WARNER.

after, but released before *Sunset Boulevard*. Wilder was less interested in her than in the three principal roles, requiring only that the part be filled with an actress of pleasing, but unremarkable looks, yet possessed with an air of youthful eagerness and intelligence, qualities she met with ease.

The women in Billy Wilder films tend to be strong in character, driving the plot forward, while the men, Joe Gillis among them, are carried along. Betty Schaefer may be a beginner alongside Norma Desmond, but she is intelligent and a fast learner. In the early scene in Sheldrake's office, she demolishes Joe's screenplay with the scalpel thrust: 'Just a rehash of something that wasn't very good to begin with.' It is exactly the succinct, disparaging judgement Sheldrake wants, and it is with malicious humour he points out that the writer is present. She then makes much of her embarrassment, and recovers adroitly. She comments that his script was not worthy of his talent.

Betty becomes attracted to Joe Gillis mainly because he *is* a writer, and she has not been around long enough to have met the bigger names. She is ambitious for her time. Today she would have her sights set on becoming a production executive herself, but she is imprisoned in the world of 1950, when a woman's ambition in the film industry was limited to the marrying and influencing of powerful men. Her interest in Joe is conditional on his success, which she believes she can stimulate. In a sense she is self-deluding, like Norma, believing that she can make something of the weak Joe. On looking at another of his scripts she feels that there is an idea that can be developed from it. After an

accidental meeting or two a relationship develops, albeit in a clandestine, but innocent manner. Their nocturnal scriptwriting sessions in her office in the Paramount Writers' Building are punctuated by strolls around the deserted lot where the Washington Square set for *The Heiress* still stands, and they exchange life stories. It spells the betrayal by both of them of the blameless and absent Artie, respectively her fiancé and Joe's best friend, but worse, far worse, is the deception by Joe of the half-suspecting Norma, the kindling for the ensuing tragedy.

One of the aspects of *Sunset Boulevard* that makes it so daring and compelling is that for a story set in a world of artifice and illusion it has a high degree of verisimilitude, the telling of a story with exactness of observation. The film studios are not fictitious, but demonstrably Paramount, with Cecil B DeMille on the real Stage 18, making the real *Samson and Delilah*. The studio reconstruction of Schwab's, the famous pharmacy on Sunset Boulevard, is accurate down to the last detail. At Artie's New Year party the song *Buttons and Bows* is being sung and played by its real composer-lyricist team, Jay Livingston and Ray Evans. Joe initially lives in the recognizable Alto-Nido apartments, giving the audience its correct address. After visiting Morino, his agent, on the Bel-Air golf course, he correctly drives out of Stone Canyon Road opposite the UCLA campus, and turns east on Sunset. At the Beverly Glen traffic signals he is spotted by the finance company men who make a U-turn to pursue him. A subsequent shot shows his 1946 Plymouth convertible racing round the curve past Charing Cross Road, which would have

BELOW WILDER WITH THE COLUMNIST SIDNEY SKOLSKY AND WILLIAM HOLDEN ON THE SCHWAB'S DRUGSTORE SET.

BELOW RIGHT THE REAL SUNSET BOULEVARD INSTITUTION.

been logical. A few seconds later he has a blow out and pulls off the highway into a driveway. It is approximately where Carolwood Drive now runs south, in the 10000 block and a few yards short of the boundary between Holmby Hills and Beverly Hills. It is feasibly where a house numbered 10086 could have stood (alas, like 221B Baker Street, no such number exists). Such geographical exactitude is rare in films, it being easier to shoot without following true routes. Much innocent amusement can be had by watching the bizarre sequence of places passed on car journeys if the city concerned is a familiar one.

An insider would not have faulted *Sunset Boulevard* for the accuracy of its

background. The view of its superficial glamour from the lower rung occupied by Joe Gillis is particularly well-defined. His one-room apartment and well-used typewriter derive from Wilder's early days at the Chateau Marmont, where he too learned the wiles of dodging automobile repossessors. It is an inspired touch to incorporate Schwab's,

possibly the most famous example of the almost defunct great American institution, the neighbourhood drugstore, where it was possible to buy the morning paper, make a few phone calls with the change, lunch on a hamburger and coffee and round everything off with antacid tablets from the pharmacy counter. Schwab's was a Hollywood landmark, a familiar industry hang-out for writers and actors, and residents from the restaurantless Chateau Marmont across the street who would breakfast there. It was remodelled in the 1950s and lingered until the 1980s when it was forced to close.

That Gillis's agent should use his time on the Bel-Air golf course rather than serving his clients is another accurate shaft of Wilderian cynicism. Similarly, the sardonic scene in Sheldrake's office in which the writer has to pitch his story in a couple of sentences is an enduring element of Hollywood working practice, with its counterpart in the opening scene of Robert Altman's *The Player* of forty-two years later.

Then there is the film *noir* style, deliberately chosen by Wilder for *Sunset Boulevard*, but already becoming unfashionable. A distinctive 1940s genre identifying a mood of pessimism, foreboding, anxiety and tension, there would often be an unwholesome sexual liaison at its centre. The discernible characteristics of *noir* – dark and shadowy sets, expressionist lighting, unexpected camera angles, rain, night, sudden death, a tarnished hero on the path to destruction, a man's

LEFT SCHWAB'S AT 8024 SUNSET IN 1949. EXTENSIVELY REFURBISHED IN THE 1950S, IT FINALLY CLOSED IN 1983.

voice-over narrating – are all there in Wilder's gothic classic, which is like an elegy not just to the era of Norma Desmond, but to film *noir* itself.

The cinematographer John Seitz, a veteran of silent days who had shot Valentino in *The Four Horsemen of the Apocalypse*, had worked with Wilder before, being responsible for the powerful visual impact of *Double Indemnity* and *The Lost Weekend*, and he was accomplished at lighting *noir* set-ups. He was often the recipient of Wilder's on-set witticisms. When he asked the director how he wanted the night-time burial of the monkey in the garden to be lit, Wilder replied: 'Just give me your usual monkey-funeral shot.'

A sneak preview in Poughkeepsie, New York with the revised opening sequence, was highly successful. The audience indicated on their response cards that they now accepted it for what it was meant to be, a Hollywood tragedy. Advance screenings to the press had been enthusiastic. Paramount, in deference to the clamour in Hollywood, mounted a screening in their own projection theatre to which senior figures at other studios were invited, as well as Wilder and members of the cast. Barbara Stanwyck, Wilder's star of *Double Indemnity*, made the extraordinary gesture of kissing the hem of Swanson's skirt, while expressing admiration for her performance. Edith Head, Paramount's famous and brilliant costume designer who created her spectacular outfits for the film sent Swanson a note a day or two later: 'Dear Gloria – You should never have left – Paramount is a very dead place – and we miss you.'

But there were some voices of dissent from those who felt that the ingrates,

Brackett and Wilder, had viciously gnawed the hand that had fed them so well. In particular, Louis B Mayer, the formidable head of MGM, stood outside the theatre after the screening, angrily denouncing Wilder to his audience of sycophants, for portraying Hollywood in what he regarded as a harsh and despicable fashion. Wilder walked over to the group, and Mayer turned and poured invective at him, describing him as a disgrace who ought to be thrown out of the industry. 'I said to him "fuck you",' said Wilder. Never in history had anyone dared to address the omnipotent Mayer in such a way and expect to survive. There was an embarrassed silence and people melted away, including the livid mogul. It was a turning point, the harbinger of Mayer's downfall. Within twelve months his unabated reign at MGM from 1924 was finally over, and Dore Schary took control of the studio.

The world premiere of *Sunset Boulevard* took place without ceremony in New York, on 11 August 1950, at the Radio City Music Hall, the largest movie theatre in the world,

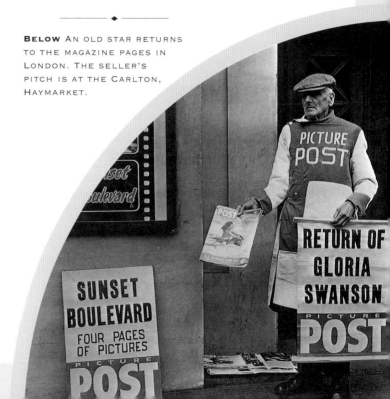

BELOW AN OLD STAR RETURNS TO THE MAGAZINE PAGES IN LONDON. THE SELLER'S PITCH IS AT THE CARLTON, HAYMARKET.

which was filled to capacity on opening day. The critics were highly approving. *The New York Times* wrote: 'Sunset Boulevard is that rare blend of pungent writing, expert acting, masterly direction and unobtrusively artistic photography which quickly casts a spell over an audience and holds it enthralled to a shattering climax.'

The London opening, unusually, followed very quickly and provided the Carlton Haymarket (now the MGM) with its biggest business for four years. Gloria Swanson faced excited British fans, and the British critics were almost unanimously enthusiastic. Dilys Powell summed up the tone when she wrote in *The Sunday Times*: 'Sunset Boulevard is the most intelligent film to come out of Hollywood for years; lest the idea of intelligence in the cinema should lack allure, let me say that it is also one of the most exciting.' The American critic James Agee, writing in *Sight and Sound*, the only serious British film magazine at that time, said: 'It is one of those rare movies which are so full of exactness, cleverness, mastery, pleasure, and arguable and unarguable choice and judgment, that they can be talked about, almost shot for shot and line for line for hours on end.'

Wilder, and Brackett, who had now ceased to be partners, were extraordinarily fortunate in their choice of star. Swanson knew how to conduct herself like one. She had been paid $50,000 for her performance, with $5,000 a week for over-runs on the schedule. Her contract required her to give publicity interviews, and she fulfilled her side with absolute professionalism, embarking on a gruelling three-month tour, mostly by train, of thirty-six cities in the United States and

ABOVE THE LONDON OPENING, 1950 WITH CROWDS AWAITING STARS AT THE CARLTON, HAYMARKET. BRITISH AUDIENCES WERE ENTHUSIASTIC.

———————— ◆ ————————

Canada, and in each accomplishing not only one-to-one interviews with the press, but appearing on radio and television, and speaking to assemblies of local worthies. Far from focusing attention all on herself she went out of her way to emphasize that the artistic success of the film stemmed from superb teamwork. She was anxious, too, that wrong conclusions should not be drawn from her screen reappearance. An extract from one of her speeches gives hints of her concern:

'It may be odd that it gives me such pride that one of the reasons Miss Olsen is so appealing, so fresh, and as utterly understandable is that she is seen in contrast to me...

as a decadent, desperate woman who has never forgiven the motion picture industry, the public or the calendar for forgetting her… and this as good a time as any to state emphatically that the story is not biographical.'

It has to be remembered that Gloria Swanson had then only recently entered her fifties, and was by no means approaching her dotage. Today actresses such as Barbra Streisand, Jane Fonda or Faye Dunaway have passed the half-century mark yet are still capable of projecting the astral glamour expected of them. Forty years ago the working life of a star was shorter, the advent of talking pictures and the Second World War having provided barriers to the advancement

of careers in many cases. Swanson appeared older because she was outside the experience of the young majority of filmgoers, and known merely as a name evoked by parents.

She relished the rebirth of her celebrity, even to the extent of appearing on the television panel game, *Twenty Questions*. But she was careful to eliminate stress, and wrote to Max Youngstein at Paramount in New York, who rejoiced in the title of Director of National Advertising, Publicity and Exploitation, about avoiding the signs that could lead to a nervous breakdown. Wednesdays, Saturdays and Sunday had to be left free. A typical two-day schedule for a publicity junket is contained in a letter to her from Jerry Juroe, a Paramount publicist outlining her programme in Los Angeles: it read…

BELOW SWANSON IN HER FINALE COSTUME, WHICH LIKE THE OTHERS WAS DESIGNED SUPERBLY BY EDITH HEAD.

DAY 1

10AM	BRUNCH WITH PRESS
12	LUNCH WITH FEDERATION OF WOMEN'S CLUBS
3PM	RADIO INTERVIEW KYA
4	RADIO INTERVIEW KGO
4.45	RADIO PROGRAM KFRC
8.30	RADIO PROGRAM (NETWORKED) KNBC

DAY 2

9AM	RADIO INTERVIEW KNBC
10	VISIT TO PARAMOUNT EXCHANGE (RENTERS)
12.15PM	RADIO INTERVIEW KCBS
2.30	TV PROGRAM KPIX
7.30	DINNER SPEECH

She set out the rules for the conduct of interviews she expected to be followed when she reached the New York stage of her tour:

1½ hours to prepare • 2 hours for hairdresser
List finishes at 4.30pm • ½ hour rest in middle of day
No dinner appointments • Vary restaurants, prefer
Pavilion, 21 and Colony • 25-word thumbnail on
everyone interviewing

She would be presented with an index card containing a brief, often cutting description ('dull, unimaginative', 'little to say') of the journalist who was to be ushered into her presence. Usually it would add the welcome note: 'He (she) is crazy about *Sunset Boulevard* '.

One of the most touching aspects of Swanson's determined professional approach was the manner in which she responded to the nice things that were being said about her. All over the United States long-service branch managers and sales-force members of the Paramount distribution arm were astonished to receive personal letters from her, addressing them as dear colleagues and recalling the days when they sold her old movies in the 1920s, and how pleasurable it was to be working with them again. The age of the word processor and photo-copier was not to dawn for decades; each letter had to be separately prepared and given those personal touches.

She had received many ecstatic reviews, and she took the trouble to write to many of the more influential critics, thanking them. It is not something that stars normally do; in general they prefer to keep their critics at a healthy distance. Swanson did not send out form letters, either. Each one was separately drafted and personally addressed, and in the majority of cases she had never met the recipients, who must have been simultaneously charmed and flabbergasted. An example of her approach is the letter to Bosley Crowther of *The New York Times*, dated 19 September 1950, which read:

> *It is all wonderful, and exciting and perhaps even still a bit giddy. I suppose I'll get used to it again before long but, believe me, in the interim I am terribly grateful to you. . . and terribly humble at the prospect of my career's renaissance.*

Surprisingly, in spite of the adulatory reception to her performance, the career renaissance turned out to be stillborn. At the Academy Awards, having earned her third nomination (although the bulk of her career had occurred before their inception) she was pipped by Judy Holliday for *Born Yesterday*. The offers that came in were for grotesque reprises of Norma Desmond, so she turned to the stage. An ill-judged film, *Three for Bedroom C* was a failure, so was *Nero's Mistress*, which she made in Italy four years later. The last of her screen appearances was in the disaster movie, *Airport 1975*, in which she played herself. She died in 1983 at the age of eighty-four.

The career of her co-star, William Holden, flourished after *Sunset Boulevard*.

After winning his Oscar for Wilder's *Stalag 17* he appeared in several hits: Wilder's *Sabrina* with Audrey Hepburn, *The Country Girl* with Grace Kelly, *Love is a Many-Splendored Thing* with Jennifer Jones, *Picnic* with Kim Novak, and David Lean's *The Bridge on the River Kwai*. For five years he was among the top ten box-office stars and in 1956 was in the number one position. He became a multi-millionaire, making sporadic appearances in his later career, such as in Peckinpah's *The Wild Bunch* and Lumet's *Network*. He also became an alcoholic, and was found dead in his apartment in 1981, apparently having fallen some days earlier.

In the 1950 Academy Awards *Sunset Boulevard* had eleven nominations, but picked up only three Oscars; best story and screenplay for Wilder, Brackett and D M Marshman Jr, best art direction and set decoration, to Hans Dreier and John Meehan, Sam Comer and Ray Moyer, and best dramatic score, to Franz Waxman. The best picture that year was *All About Eve* and Joseph L Mankiewicz won for directing it. Billy Wilder, his partnership with Brackett ended, did not allow his career to diminish. Academy Award nominations accompanied *Stalag 17*, *Sabrina* and *Witness for the Prosecution*. He found a new writing partner with I A L Diamond; together they created the sublime *Some Like it Hot*, the second time he directed Marilyn Monroe (the first was *The Seven Year Itch*) and followed it with the Academy-Award winner, *The Apartment*. His later films included *Irma la Douce*, *Kiss Me, Stupid* and *The Front Page*. If somebody were to bankroll him he would still be making films today but he has probably grown too old to be insured, as well as having the handicap of not being successful at the box office with his last pictures. Yet Wilder at one point was the most reliable of all the studio directors, his films having grossed more than $100 million.

There was a curious, little-known aftermath to Gloria Swanson's performance in *Sunset Boulevard*. Although she had adamantly resisted offers to reprise the role or attempt anything in a similar category, in the mid-1950s she became involved in a plan to turn the story into a stage musical, which she was to star in as well as produce. The property belonged not to Billy Wilder, who had no financial interest in it whatsoever, but to Paramount, and she was encouraged to believe that they would be prepared to grant a licence. 'I shall just really be making time (with my dress business and a possible picture in Europe),' she wrote to D A Doran, a Paramount executive, 'until my dream can come true – *Sunset Boulevard* as a musical.'

The creative team was British: Dickson Hughes and Richard Stapley and Swanson made them an advance to complete the score and lyrics. 'If Gertrude Lawrence could have success with *The King and I* on Broadway, then so can I,' she observed. She did, in fact, have a firm and accurate singing voice, but the public rarely had an opportunity to hear it, except in later life when she appeared on television specials on American networks, such as that of the comedienne Carol Burnett in 1973.

The intention was to open the show in London first. Hughes and Stapley worked diligently to complete the project, making considerable changes to the story in the process, in consultation with Swanson.

Norma was no longer to be a hugely rich ex-star living off her oilwell profits, but instead was to have only pretended to have a fortune, pawning her last pieces of jewellery in order to pay for the New Year's Eve party. At the end 'boy' was to get 'girl' Joe and Betty running off united with Norma's blessing. Quite clearly, the ironic effect of Wilder's film would have been totally lost in the adaptation, which seemed to have been made with the intention of creating an anodyne entertainment as well as a vehicle for a distinguished and ageing star.

Swanson wrote to Erich von Stroheim in Paris, asking if he would consider appearing in his old part. 'These days,' she noted, 'not much is required of actors in the way of singing. Think of Paul Lukas in *Call Me Madam*.' Stroheim, probably too ill by then, declined. He died in 1957, a tragic and in his own eyes, unfulfilled genius.

In London Swanson's agents, MCA, tried to find an impresario prepared to stage it. Jack Hylton declined, pleading too many commitments, but Gerald Palmer, who had produced ice shows in various British cities with Tom Arnold, was interested. José Ferrer was canvassed as a possible director. Meanwhile Stapley and Hughes had completed their work.

Then on 20 February 1957 the labours of the preceding two years were suddenly negated. Paramount backed down on whatever assurances had been given earlier to Swanson, and refused permission for the show to be staged. 'It would be damaging for the property to be offered to the entertainment public in another form as a stage musical,' wrote Russell Holman of Paramount

ABOVE OSCAR NIGHT: JOSÉ FERRER, SWANSON, WINNER JUDY HOLLIDAY.

to her in a devastating letter. Swanson, having spent a considerable sum commissioning the work was stupefied by the refusal. The closest the show, which was to have been called *Boulevard*, ever got to the public was the performance of a song or two on television before the embargo, but recordings of the entire score are preserved in the Gloria Swanson archives at the University of Texas.

Paramount did in fact re-release *Sunset Boulevard* in 1960 to the next film-going generation. It is now generally regarded as one of the two great films from several hundreds that have been made about Hollywood. The other being the light-hearted, but bitingly satirical, musical on the transition of silent pictures into talkies, Gene Kelly and Stanley Donen's *Singin' in the Rain*, which came out two years after *Sunset Boulevard*, in 1952. In the succeeding years Wilder's film was to become familiar through frequent showings on television. Its reputation has survived the passage of time and its potency remains undiminished. Hooray for Hollywood.

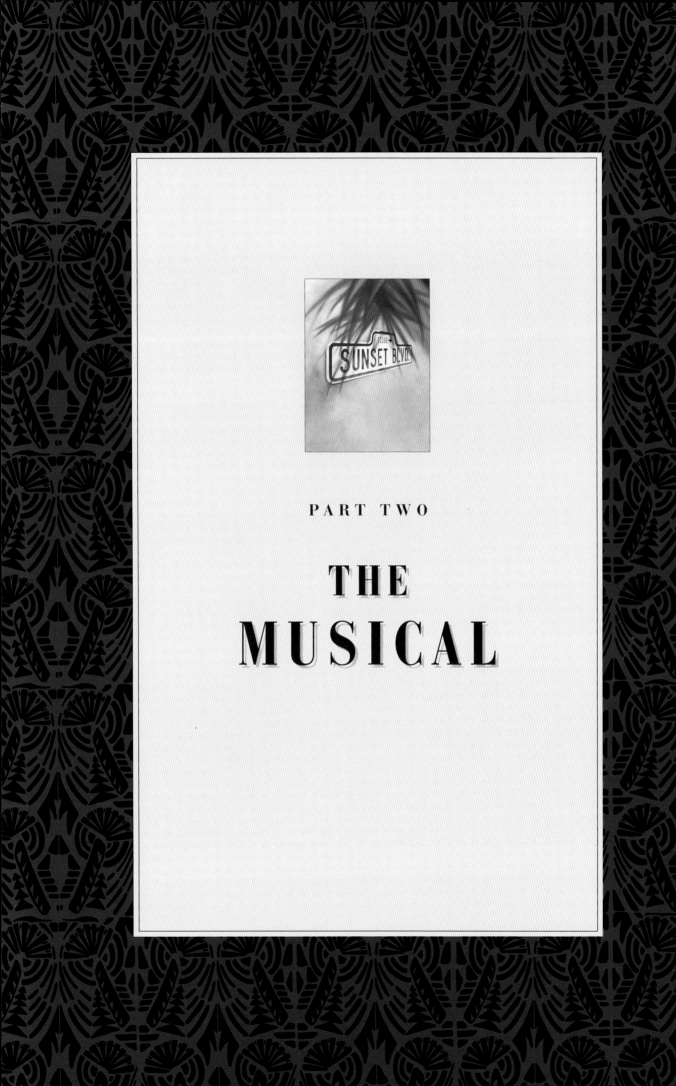

PART TWO

THE
MUSICAL

A   B R I T I S H   I N I T I A T I V E

TREVOR NUNN (DIRECTOR)

ANDREW LLOYD
WEBBER
(COMPOSER)

JOHN NAPIER
(PRODUCTION
DESIGNER)

CHRISTOPHER
HAMPTON
(CO-WRITER)

PATTI
LuPONE
(NORMA
DESMOND)

DON BLACK
(CO-WRITER)

KEVIN
ANDERSON
(JOE GILLIS)

ABOVE THE CREATIVE TEAM FOR *SUNSET BOULEVARD* –
THE MUSICAL

Although it was at almost the last moment in its progress towards the stage that Gloria Swanson's attempt to turn *Sunset Boulevard* into a musical was thwarted by Paramount, in retrospect the decision can be regarded as having been aesthetically correct. Her version, with its manufactured happy ending and other drastic changes, would inevitably have damaged the integrity of Billy Wilder's film. Wilder, not owning the copyright of the screenplay, was unprotected from numerous ensuing bids to adapt and alter his work for other attempted musicals. After the 1960 re-release of the film, Paramount appeared to have no further reservations over stage adaptations and the rights passed into various hands, but all failed to achieve their goal. One of the composers interested was Stephen Sondheim.

In the early 1970s Andrew Lloyd Webber saw *Sunset Boulevard* but now cannot precisely remember the circumstances, only the effect it had on him. 'I realized then that there was something that could be turned into a musical,' he recalled, 'but at that time I was very caught up with my ill-fated production of *Jeeves* and after that, *Evita*, and it was one of those things that went on to the back burner.'

Andrew Lloyd Webber's achievements are unparalleled in the history of British and American musical theatre. He was knighted in 1992 for services to the arts at the relatively youthful age of forty-four, following his phenomenal success. In 1982 and again in 1988 he became the first composer to have three musicals running simultaneously in London and New York, and in 1991 broke another record with six shows running concurrently in the West End. There have been periods when twenty per cent of the box-office takings of all London theatres, the greatest concentration of playhouses in the world, have been for the shows of Andrew

Lloyd Webber. He has used his vast wealth to develop his interest in Victorian art and has become a world authority on the pre-Raphaelites as well as amassing an outstanding collection of their paintings which he hopes eventually to house in a gallery for the benefit of Britain.

He was born in 1948, the son of William Lloyd Webber, the former head of the London College of Music, and was a scholar at Westminster School. From there he won a History Exhibition to Magdalen College, Oxford, but left during his freshman year to study at the Royal College of Music. Here he embarked on what was to become one of the most celebrated collaborations in musical theatre, with the lyricist Tim Rice who was four years older and at that stage working for the EMI recording company. The first performance of a one-act musical, *Joseph and the Amazing Technicolor Dreamcoat*, based on the Bible story and wittily incorporating various pop-song idioms, was staged at Colet Court prep school in West London in 1968, and was seen by Derek Jewell, a perceptive music critic of *The Sunday Times* who immediately realized he was watching exceptional young talent. His positive and encouraging review was their first national recognition.

Their initial West End show, *Jesus Christ Superstar*, was established on stage by the then unprecedented ploy of recording and releasing the entire score as an album long in advance. Meanwhile *Joseph* was rewritten to become a full-length show, and the culmination of the Lloyd Webber-Rice collaboration was *Evita*, a musical biography of Eva Peron, the wife of the Argentinian dictator. Their partnership then went into abeyance.

Ever since, a stream of Lloyd Webber hits has permanently occupied a large proportion of the West End and Broadway stages, including *Cats, Starlight Express, The Phantom of the Opera* and *Aspects of Love*, the latter adjudged a relative failure in Lloyd Webber terms since it ran for under four years. His theatrical interests are tended by a division of the Really Useful Group, his own company that is now in part owned by Polygram since a shrewd deal in 1991.

While *Evita* was being staged in London in 1976 its American director, Harold Prince, raised with Lloyd Webber the question of creating a musical from *Sunset Boulevard*, and revealed that he had acquired the rights. 'When Evita was up and running in the West End,' said Lloyd Webber, 'Hal suggested that I should go over to New York to have a chat about it. He didn't have any idea about the lyrics, but thought that Hugh Wheeler – he's dead now – should do the book. The idea was to make the whole thing hark back to the early Fifties. Hal seemed to have the idea of it being more about a Doris Day figure than a Norma Desmond silent star. To be honest, I was not terribly keen to tamper with the film, and equally I couldn't really clear my decks to do it, so it remained in limboland.'

Then followed a coincidence. Tim Rice was at school at Lancing, and his contemporaries included the embryonic playwrights David Hare and Christopher Hampton. During an informal lunch Lloyd Webber had with Christopher Hampton to sound out the possibilities of a future collaboration, the playwright told him that were he ever to turn to a musical the subject that held the most fascination for him was *Sunset Boulevard*.

Said Lloyd Webber: 'I tucked that piece of information away because *Cats* had by that time overtaken things, and *Starlight* came quickly after that, and I was doing the *Requiem Mass* and getting a divorce, and very quickly after that came *Phantom* – I was working on an awful lot in a very short period, and I rather forgot about it, until after *Aspects* which had also taken a long time to do. It was only after *Aspects* that I thought that the *Sunset* idea had been hanging around for far too long, and I wondered if

ABOVE TREVOR NUNN CONFERS WITH THE *SUNSET BOULEVARD* WRITERS, DON BLACK AND CHRISTOPHER HAMPTON

Chris Hampton was really serious about working on it. I had a preliminary talk with him, and he said "I'm rather frightened at writing lyrics, I haven't done that before." Then I met up with a young American lyricist, Amy Powers, who did a few bits and pieces for me, which we tried out. She was not untalented, but young and a little over-awed by the whole thing.'

Lloyd Webber realized that somebody with more experience would need to become involved. 'I could totally understand that Christopher wanted to work with a lyricist because if you are doing a musical for the first time you want to work with somebody who at least knows how you deliver say, the main arias, with the proper titles. So I thought, why not introduce him to Don Black? I had worked with Don several times before, and I knew that Don is particularly sensitive to women, as in *Tell Me on a Sunday*, and would understand what made Norma Desmond tick. So they met and decided to collaborate, at which point we pushed the button. Working with Christopher Hampton has been a great eye-opener, I've never really worked with a dramatist of his calibre, not recently anyway.' In fact, Lloyd Webber's collaboration with Alan Ayckbourn for *Jeeves* in 1975 resulted in his only flop.

Don Black, born in Hackney, East London in 1938, has had a multi-faceted working life, ranging from promoting a pop music magazine to being an agent and manager for Brian Epstein and even spending a couple of years as a stand-up comedian. As a lyricist, his first chart hit was the ballad 'Walk Away' which established the career of the silky-voiced singer Matt Monro, formerly a London bus driver, and it reached No. 2 in the United Kingdom charts. On the strength of its success Don Black was hired to write film theme songs, winning an Oscar for his lyrics to John Barry's theme for *Born Free*. He has also had four other Academy Award nominations. He wrote the lyrics for the James Bond films *Thunderball*, *Diamonds are Forever* and *The Man With the Golden Gun* and for the theme song of *To Sir With Love*, a No. 1 hit for Lulu. Another No. 1 on both sides of the Atlantic was Michael Jackson's 'Ben', allegedly the superstar's favourite song. Black's debut as a lyricist for a West End show was with *Billy*, starring Michael Crawford and his first Lloyd Webber collaboration was the song cycle *Tell Me on a Sunday* which evolved into the show *Song and Dance*. Later, he wrote the lyrics for *Aspects of Love*, helping to establish Michael Ball as a star with 'Love Changes Everything'.

Lloyd Webber had first discussed his thoughts on *Sunset Boulevard* with Don Black in 1979 after *Tell Me on a Sunday* and following a viewing of the film they even mapped out a couple of songs. One of them, a theme for Norma Desmond, was called 'One Star' and Lloyd Webber later used the tune as a basis for 'Memory' in *Cats*.

The background of Christopher Hampton is very different. He was born in the Azores in 1946, where his father worked for Cable & Wireless and, after a peripatetic childhood and school at Lancing, graduated in 1968 from New College, Oxford, with a degree in modern languages. He then became resident dramatist at the Royal Court Theatre, London. His original plays include *The Philanthropist*, *The Savages* and *Tales from Hollywood*, but he has also excelled in adaptation and translation of works by Ibsen, Molière, Chekhov and the dramatization of the epistolary novel by Choderlos de Laclos, *Les Liaisons Dangereuses* which he further adapted for the Stephen Frears film, *Dangerous Liaisons*, winning the 1988 Academy Award for best screenplay. His interest in *Sunset Boulevard* stemmed from his research for *Tales from Hollywood* which brought him into contact with Billy Wilder.

The partnership with Don Black, seen in some quarters as an egghead meeting Tin Pan Alley, proved fruitful and fulfilling on both sides. 'We got on rather well, and quickly discovered that we had a similar sense of humour,' said Hampton. Their respective talents, although contrasted, proved compatible, creating a sort of synergy as they worked. 'The movie is a masterpiece,' said Don Black, 'a lyric writer's dream, there was so much to work on.'

They found themselves in total accord that it would not be a show punctuated with elaborate production numbers, the stage filled with a huge cast singing and dancing. Each song would have to arise organically from the plot, with its logic carefully delineated.

'It was originally,' said Lloyd Webber speaking of the way *Sunset* was to be credited, 'going to be book by Christopher Hampton, lyrics by Don Black, music by me. But then very interesting things happened, and at their request the credit is now "book and lyrics by Don Black and Christopher Hampton". Some of the later lyrics I would have thought were not by Don Black because I know him too well, yet I know that really they are. It is a genuine collaboration.'

At one stage there had been a fleeting possibility of a revival of the Tim Rice-Andrew Lloyd Webber partnership. 'There was,' said Lloyd Webber, 'serious discussion of Tim becoming involved, although early on when I talked about it to him, he didn't particularly respond to the piece. He felt that the characters were not all that sympathetic, for one thing. He also said that he didn't think there should be a song in it called 'Sunset Boulevard' and I rather thought that there should. But the other problem was that I had already talked to Don, and I had also talked to Chris a long time before, and Tim is not somebody who would relish somebody else coming into the mix.' The chances, however, of a future collaboration are, he insists, not hopeless; it is a question of them finding a mutually suitable subject.

During the first discussions on *Sunset Boulevard* Christopher Hampton readily concurred with Lloyd Webber's view that the original story should be adhered to as closely as possible, even to the retention of lines that were used in the film and which, over the years, have found their way into the folklore of the movies. For instance, when Joe first

recognizes Norma Desmond and tactlessly blurts out 'You used to be big,' causing her to retort 'I *am* big. It's the pictures that got small' her line is so famous and widely quoted (or misquoted, since it is popularly and erroneously thought to be 'I'm *still* big', altering the sense and balance of the thought) that a stage production of *Sunset Boulevard* without it seems almost unthinkable.

The eventual script for the show contained much more dialogue than in most Lloyd Webber musicals, with some twenty per cent of the lines spoken rather than sung, although there is underscoring almost throughout. A possible area of difficulty was the necessity to construct dialogue in the spirit of Wilder and Brackett's screenplay that would blend in with the retained lines from the film yet advance the story and enable the transitions into song to be achieved seamlessly.

'As a dramatist,' said Hampton, 'I had to get used to the pacing, and learn that when a song is used to make a plot point it will usually take rather longer to get it across than a spoken line can in a play.'

Said Don Black: 'Christopher was always much more logical than me, and he would insist that the tone was always right, that the words would belong to the person singing them, be right for the character, and not veer off. This was not a show full of big numbers and dance routines, but really just a piece about four or five people.'

BELOW KEVIN ANDERSON AND PATTI LUPONE REHEARSE

Their method of working was to listen constantly to a piano recording of Andrew Lloyd Webber playing the melody, not through an expensive stereo system but on Don Black's cheap Japanese cassette player, and then to fit the words to it. When ideas occurred for numbers they would try them on the composer. 'I remember,' said Hampton, 'how we needed a song to arise out of the scene in which Max projects one of Norma Desmond's old films. We discussed it with Andrew, and the following morning he played us the music for Norma's song, 'New Ways to Dream', which is later reprised by Max.'

Said Lloyd Webber: 'That was practically the last thing I wrote for it; at the very eleventh hour I came up with a theme that was worth putting words to just before we did the festival at Sydmonton.'

Tim Rice's criticism that the characters were unsympathetic was always taken seriously. As Andrew Lloyd Webber put it, it was undesirable that the audience should leave the theatre 'thinking who cares about an old woman who's a faded star and too rich anyway, and a boy who's on the make – and fake.' Looking closer at the inter-relationships of the four main characters, he began to sense that Betty would have to be built up and made softer, with Artie, a relatively shadowy figure in the film, being drawn more into the centre, so that his betrayal by his best friend generates a stronger emotional ache.

Early on, the creative trio decided that the curtain scene at the end of the first half should be the New Year party in Artie's apartment, with Joe telephoning Max asking him to pack his things so that he can move out and stay with his friend. It is the moment

ABOVE THE YOUNG HOPEFULS IN REHEARSAL FOR THE NEW YEAR'S EVE PARTY

in which Joe learns that Norma has slashed her wrists, thus causing him to abandon the party and his plan, and to race back to 10086 Sunset Boulevard. Dramatically, it was the counterpart of the final curtain, his decision to purge himself totally, not only of Norma but also of Betty and to clear out of Hollywood for good – the point at which Norma, in madness, shoots him. 'It is possible to make Norma a great deal more sympathetic. Music can do that for you, it can make you get underneath her soul,' says Lloyd Webber.

The composer has a tendency to file information and ideas away in what he calls his memory bank while getting on with other projects, recalling these when a need arises. 'The one song that I had used before in any guise was the title song, 'Sunset Boulevard' itself, which I could never find a proper home for, or make work properly. It was written around about the time of *Jesus Christ Superstar* and it was intended to be a song about movies. Then I wanted it to be the theme tune of Stephen Frears's film *Gumshoe* which I was scoring, made in about 1971, but it didn't work. It didn't become the theme, although sleuths may recognize that there are a couple of fragments in the film score.'

They are discernible. 'One night I decided to watch *Gumshoe* on television,' said Christopher Hampton, 'and there in a railway station scene where Albert Finney and Billie Whitelaw are saying goodbye, there for about thirty seconds is our song, without its beginning and end, but quite recognizable.' It has now been transformed, and opens the second act, sung bitterly by Joe:

Sunset Boulevard
twisting Boulevard
secretive and rich, a little scary.

Sunset Boulevard
tempting Boulevard
waiting there to swallow the unwary.

'I think,' said Lloyd Webber, 'that *Sunset Boulevard* is the only musical that can claim to have its title song in 5/8 time. There's a restlessness with that time signature. I was pleased to have found a home for my little song, rather like Richard Rodgers when he eventually found a home for the *Carousel* overture, which he had written years earlier.'

Work progressed. Public interest was roused when the newspapers reported that the next big Lloyd Webber musical was to be *Sunset Boulevard*.

The press's response to the early announcements was to generate stories on 'who will play Norma Desmond?' lines. Various names were speculatively mentioned, and Meryl Streep, one of the earlier contenders for the lead in the film version of *Evita*, still languishing unmade after several years, was soon regarded as the front-runner.

Enlivening the late summer each year at Sydmonton, the 4,000-acre Lloyd Webber country estate on the Hampshire-Berkshire border, is a three-day music festival, with events staged within a small, ancient church in the grounds. It has often been the setting for early demonstrations of work in progress, and within its walls several Lloyd Webber shows have received their first performances in workshop conditions. The highlight of the Sydmonton Festival in September 1992 was a complete performance of *Sunset Boulevard* in the state it had reached by that time, with most of the score and book already limned sufficiently to enable a cast to present it effectively on the tiny stage.

The role of Norma Desmond was sung by Patti LuPone, one of Broadway's most distinguished performers and the winner of a Tony for her lead in the New York production of *Evita* and a nomination as Reno Sweeney

LEFT KEVIN ANDERSON DELIVERS THE TITLE SONG

ABOVE PATTI LUPONE
IN HER TOWELLING POOLSIDE ROBE

in the 1988 revival of Cole Porter's *Anything Goes*. When she sang the first big solo, 'With One Look', the acoustic effect in the tiny building was electrifying, and it was clear at the end of the evening that those present had witnessed one of the longest auditions in history rewarded with success. Some present were moved to tears, including Meryl Streep, and cynics in the press suggested that it was not so much that she was moved by the emotional intensity of LuPone's performance but by the realization that the race to play Norma Desmond for the world premiere in the following summer was over.

Opposite Patti LuPone in the role of Joe was Kevin Anderson, a young actor from Chicago who at that time was best known for playing Julia Roberts' rescuer in the film *Sleeping With the Enemy*. He too passed the

'audition'; some time later when watching the Sydmonton video, the director of the stage version of *Sunset Boulevard*, Trevor Nunn, who had not been present at the live performance, declared that he need look no further.

There was still much work to be done on the script. An early ensemble number, cleverly intended to establish the false bonhomie prevailing in the Hollywood working community, was called 'Let's Do Lunch', a common phrase as insincere and meaningless as 'have a nice day'. Alas, research established that nobody 'did' lunch in 1950 and it was later changed to the less resonant but non-anachronistic 'Let's Have Lunch.' The biggest alteration after Sydmonton concerned the New Year's Eve party which, in order to make something of a spectacular set, was in the earlier version to be held on the soundstage of DeMille's *Samson and Delilah* with Cecil B himself playing host to all his underlings. Later it was realized that there was a fundamental illogicality about it; the last thing the haughty DeMille would do on his New Year's Eve would be to spend it in the company of a horde of young people less than half his age, and many of them his employees. The scene was consequently restored to Artie's apartment, with one of the guests performing a mocking impersonation.

**SAMMY: Behold, my children,
it is I, Cecil B DeMille,
meeting me must be quite a thrill,
ADAM: but there's no need to kneel.**

**SAMMY: I guarantee you
every girl in my chorus line
is a genuine philistine
SANDY: they don't come off the shelf
SAMMY: I flew everyone in from Philistia myself.**

LEFT CINEMATIC
CROSS-CUTTING – NORMA'S HOUSE
AND ARTIE'S APARTMENT
ON STAGE AT THE SAME TIME

BELOW THE CROWDED PARTY
IN ARTIE'S APARTMENT

Observed Lloyd Webber: 'If all our young hopefuls had been going to a studio bash, they would have all been in tuxedos in those days, and the arrival of Joe in tails would have been ineffective. But the advantage of staging the scene in Artie's apartment is that it provided me with two wondrous musical and dramatic ingredients. I have this little band that plays on inexorably in Norma Desmond's house, and at the same time the young people are having fun at their party. You see both simultaneously, and there are two musical ingredients on the stage that cross-fade. The audience must not be too aware that we have done something on the stage that in film can be done terribly easily, the cross-fade. It's a great theatrical challenge, the young people all crushed together contrasted with the complete emptiness of Norma's house.'

The young people's song, played at the party, 'This Time Next Year' has a lively, mambo beat recognizable as a pop idiom of the early 1950s, and the witty lyrics describe the career ambitions of the hopefuls, even managing to incorporate a reference to the film's creator:

MARY: I'll be discovered
my life won't ever be the same
Billy Wilder will know my name
and he'll call all the time
KATHERINE: till he does can one of you guys lend her a dime?

Said Christopher Hampton: 'We added that thought after Sydmonton when the verses were sharpened up to make more of the location change.' A preceding scene, 'The Lady's Paying,' the stage variation of the film sequence in which Joe is outfitted by Norma in expensive new togs at an upmarket menswear store, takes place in the musical at the mansion, with an entire phalanx of supercilious assistants led by an unctuous head salesman carrying in shirts, ties, socks, shoes, suits, evening wear and the exquisite vicuna overcoat. It is used as a means of effecting Joe's quick change into tails for Norma's New Year party. 'We've set it up,' said Andrew Lloyd Webber, 'with Norma leaving Joe with the salesmen, so it becomes Joe versus them, and then she reappears and starts picking out stuff for him, and leaves again, and they say it's worth the price, because the lady's paying.

We thought it more logical that they would come to Norma Desmond, to her house. It then makes her journey to Paramount in the second act possibly her first visit out for twenty years.'

Trevor Nunn was appointed director in early December 1992 and John Napier the production designer. Nunn, born in 1940 and a graduate of Downing College, Cambridge, became the youngest artistic director of the Royal Shakespeare Company in 1968, and continued to run it until 1986. His earlier Andrew Lloyd Webber productions included *Cats*, *Starlight Express* and *Aspects of Love*. He also directed *Les Misérables* which won eight Tony awards. John Napier, an associate designer for the Royal Shakespeare Company, studied at the Hornsey College of Art and the Central School of Arts and Crafts, and his musicals include Andrew Lloyd Webber's

ABOVE REHEARSING 'THE LADY'S PAYING' –
JOE GETS NEW CLOTHES

Cats and *Starlight Express*, and *Miss Saigon* and *Les Misérables*. He was also the production designer on Steven Spielberg's film *Hook*.

Every Tuesday evening Trevor Nunn would meet the two writers and Andrew Lloyd Webber to discuss each scene, and its problems of staging. For Christopher Hampton, more accustomed to the isolation of playwriting, the disciplines of working within a team seemed similar to working on a

ABOVE TREVOR NUNN CALLS THE SHOTS

movie. 'Our exchanges were often lively, and I probably had more disagreements with Trevor than with anyone else, although he was more often or not right in the end. Andrew used to sit and watch our arguments with amusement. I suppose if things were really difficult it was he who made the decision in the end.'

'It was very democratic,' said Nunn, 'a regular ritual endeavour, and in my experience the material was changed less than during the usual run-up to the staging of a show.'

One of the biggest problems in adapting a familiar movie to a dramatic performance on a stage was what to do with those sequences that required outdoor action. Film, unfettered by the confines of the theatre, can incorporate sequences in which characters travel from one location to another as part of the plot. One such key moment occurs near the start of Wilder's film when Joe is on his way back from the fruitless meeting with his agent at the Bel-Air Country Club, and is spotted by the automobile repossessors at a traffic light. In the ensuing car chase along Sunset Boulevard he has the blowout that causes him to pull into Norma Desmond's driveway. Since this is the dramatic means by which the confrontation between Joe and Norma occurs it is more satisfactory that the audience should see it happen, rather than merely hear it described. Said Hampton: 'Initially Andrew was all for going out and filming things like that, and inserting them into the show. But Trevor was very much against that, saying that there had to be a theatrical answer, and he persuaded Andrew, who then told him to go off with John Napier to try to work something out.'

'It's a matter of sheer practicality,' said Nunn. 'In a film script anything is possible. There's a price to pay if the original intentions are to remain. Solutions have to involve technology, but not to overwhelm things.'

Said Lloyd Webber: 'The chase was vital to us. We could not drop the car chase, because it was the reason why Joe got to the house. Trevor and John worked in another theatre to find a technical solution. What we simply couldn't do was to put a car on the stage because it would take up two-thirds of the proscenium. I accepted that it was wrong to have some specific film shot. There is a technique, very difficult to achieve and requiring complex projection systems in which you can move an actor in and out of the film. But that would have meant taking us into high-tech areas, which I didn't think right for *Sunset*.'

The manner of solving it incorporated projected footage from the Wilder film, blown up to fill most of the stage area, a few seconds-worth of shots of the cars racing round the Holmby Hills' curves that were optically stretched, incorporating flips and zooms, and printed grainily with low contrast. Within these screened images insets open at various points like an Advent calendar to reveal the drivers, traffic lights, wheels and speedometers. The working out of the effect was not easy and had to be tested at another theatre, the Cambridge which was 'dark' at the time, in order not to interfere with rehearsals at the Adelphi. What emerged was a theatrical method of imitating rapid film editing, and similar but less elaborate techniques were evolved for later moments such as the outing of Norma Desmond's car to Paramount, and

the rainswept dash by Betty to her house.

Later in the year a videotape of the Sydmonton workshop performance was shown to Billy Wilder in Beverly Hills, and it was agreed by Really Useful that although Paramount were receiving the royalties his name would be featured prominently in the show's advertising. 'It's not money in the bank, but it's better than nothing. Anyway you eat less as you get older,' quipped Wilder. He pronounced what he saw very satisfactory. 'I congratulate Don Black and Christopher Hampton on something ingenious – they left the story alone, that's already a very ingenious idea. A woman comes forward and says "I am big. It's the pictures that got small". I was very much astonished when I heard the words, many of them retained and some of them to music. I'm not an expert on music but it sounded good to me.'

Andrew Lloyd Webber had accidentally nudged the VCR, scrambling the picture which, although eventually retrieved, was in black and white. 'Don't worry,' said Wilder, 'I prefer it like that.'

ABOVE THE CAR-CHASE MONTAGE, A FILM EFFECT ON STAGE

The decision to open the show in London on 29 June 1993 was taken even before a firm idea of its venue had been formed. Andrew Lloyd Webber's Really Useful Group had owned the Palace for a number of years, a notable Victorian theatre built by Thomas Collcutt in 1890 for Sir Arthur Sullivan as the London Opera House. In 1986 Lloyd Webber would have liked to have staged *The Phantom of the Opera* there, but Cameron Mackintosh's Royal Shakespeare Company production of *Les Misérables* was ensconced and clearly destined for a long run, so *The Phantom* went to Her Majesty's, initially with some apprehension by Lloyd Webber since it had been the scene of his rare failure, *Jeeves*.

In 1993 both shows were still cemented into their respective houses. Meanwhile Cameron Mackintosh, having taken over the Prince Edward Theatre, was spending three million pounds on its refurbishment. Lloyd

ABOVE THE SAFETY CURTAIN DROPS INSIDE THE NEW PROSCENIUM

Webber decided that it was too big for *Sunset Boulevard*, and so instead it was earmarked for Mackintosh's production of the imported American show, *Crazy for You*, with its Gershwin music and extended line of high-kicking chorus girls.

At the Adelphi the eight-year run of *Me and My Girl* was ending, and Lloyd Webber bought a half-interest in the theatre from James Nederlander, with the intention of refurbishing it for the opening of *Sunset Boulevard*. The first Adelphi had been built on the site overlooking The Strand in 1806, and at various times in its long history it had been rebuilt, in 1858, 1901 and 1930 when the Strand frontage was given a dramatic moderne treatment and the auditorium remodelled. When the theatre was reconstructed the changes were often superficial, and within the present building are remains of all its earlier incarnations. The rear of the theatre, backing on to Maiden Lane, is still rec-

BELOW THE CRAMPED STAGE AREA IS CLEARED

ognizably mid-Victorian, and it was at the old stage door, now bricked up, that one night in 1897 the actor William Terriss, the most celebrated star of the melodramatic spectacles then popular in the West End, was stabbed to death by a rival. Theatrical superstitions abound; his ghost is said to haunt the Adelphi, and there are many recorded sightings.

'Although the Adelphi has seen many big musicals over the years,' said Lloyd Webber, 'it actually has quite an intimate auditorium, and the proscenium is not very wide. It suits *Sunset* because it is really a four-hander show, with a few other characters. People would be very disappointed if they came expecting something like *Crazy for You*.'

The stage area needed the most attention, being largely unaltered since the 1858 reconstruction. The Adelphi also had a revolving stage installed in the interwar years which had become worn out and unusable.

◆

ABOVE BACKSTAGE GLIMPSES OF SETS INCLUDING THE *SAMSON AND DELILAH* SOUND STAGE

◆

Inadequate wing space is one of its serious handicaps, and some of the extravagant musicals staged there would only have been possible because of the revolve. Nevertheless, it had to be stripped out and a new stage built to modern specifications allowing heavy sets to be swiftly hoisted into the flies above and for a much larger orchestra to be accommodated in the pit. Meanwhile the auditorium and front of house were restored by the architect John Muir to the appearance of the theatre following the 1930 rebuilding to the designs of Ernest Schaufelberg, when it re-opened with Jessie Matthews and Sonnie Hale in *Ever Green*. The bold angular appearance of Schaufelberg's work had been marred in intervening years by insensitive changes which had compromised it in an attempt to make the asymmetrical auditorium more traditional; the effect was to render it dowdy. Muir chose the materials for the re-seating, carpeting and internal gold-and-tan decor as

BELOW THE OCTAGONAL WINDOW IS RESTORED IN WHAT WILL BECOME THE BILLY WILDER BAR

close to the 1930 design as possible, while altering the front-of-house layout so that the staircase to the Grand Circle (the impressive name for the upper balcony) was integrated into the main entrance rather than separately segregated as before. A huge irregular octagonal window in the dress circle bar, covered for decades by the neon advertising display, was restored, enhancing the external appearance of the theatre and bringing back a once-familiar landmark for Strand pedestrians. In the final weeks, as the opening date approached, work went on day and night to lay carpet and install the new seats.

At the beginning of May 1993 the cast assembled for the first time. There was an unfortunate gaffe on the eve of Patti LuPone's departure from New York, when it was announced, ending weeks of speculation, that the part of Norma Desmond would be played for the American premiere production by Glenn Close. The timing of the announcement could have been better-handled.

Earlier, Andrew Lloyd Webber had taken the decision that the first American production should open not on Broadway, but in Los Angeles in 1993, within six months of the world premiere in London, and that New York would see *Sunset Boulevard* in the second half of 1994, with Patti LuPone and Kevin Anderson in the leading roles. His reasoning was that the story was a Hollywood one and also that his experiences of Los Angeles productions had always been favourable, so he felt it was right that the city should have the premiere, a view the Shubert Organization was happy to accommodate, and the 1,800-seat Shubert Theatre at Century City was earmarked as the west coast venue.

Patti LuPone, honoured by being chosen as the first Norma Desmond, made no secret that she would have preferred the American opening to have been on Broadway, allowing her to score the double. 'I am, after all, a New Yorker,' she said, staunchly supporting the city in which her stardom was most recognized. She even initially wondered if Broadway might not feel put down by a Los Angeles opening. 'But everything's right in the universe, as David Mamet would say. I'm too old for any bullshit and I don't want any.'

At forty-three she was almost too young to play Norma Desmond, but was prepared to add a few years. 'I've worked in

ABOVE COMING INTO HER PRIME.
PATTI LUPONE PREPARES TO BECOME NORMA DESMOND

Hollywood, where they are obsessed with youth, the MTV generation. You reach forty in the United States and as a woman you're obsolete. They'll tell you, you're an old bag. But on the stage I now think I'm coming into my prime.

'I can relate to Norma Desmond, and the star she was, who was rejected. In my own small way I can relate to that rejection, as a woman in America, in her forties.'

The part of Betty Schaefer, played in the film by Nancy Olson, was assigned to Meredith Braun, a petite New Zealand-born actress who had appeared in the West End in the ill-fated musical *Bernadette*, and in *Les Misérables*. The casting of Max, Norma's butler, protector and one-time director and husband, proved particularly difficult, and an expedition had been mounted by Trevor Nunn to Vienna to look at east European actors. Memories of Erich von Stroheim were difficult to erase, and without his availability, having died in 1957, the final choice was Daniel Benzali, who had played General Peron on Broadway in *Evita* and had appeared on the screen several times, including in the James Bond film, *A View to a Kill* with Roger Moore.

While the builders worked frantically at the theatre to ready the stage for the cast, initial rehearsals began at the Riverside Studios in West London. The staging of the musical numbers was the responsibility of Bob Avian, a Broadway veteran who had been a dancer

ABOVE MEREDITH BRAUN, A PERT BETTY SCHAEFER, WITH KEVIN ANDERSON

in a dozen shows, including *West Side Story* and *Funny Girl*, and had then spent twenty years working with Michael Bennett, winning a Tony for his choreography for *A Chorus Line*, and a second for *Ballroom*. He and Trevor Nunn worked in parallel, blocking the cast movements.

ABOVE DANIEL BENZALI, STEPPING IN STROHEIM'S SHOES AS MAX

Meanwhile, at the Adelphi, still in the midst of its extensive refurbishment, the massive sets were being erected on the new stage. The production designer for *Sunset Boulevard*, John Napier, was an associate of the RSC who had worked in partnership with Trevor Nunn on many productions. 'There's something very intimidating in trying to put a classic film on the stage,' he said. 'At first the problems seemed insoluble, particularly given the restrictions of the theatre itself.'

His primary set, on view longer than any of the others, is the interior of Norma Desmond's mansion, a breathtakingly ornate rococo Hollywood interior, with panelled walls inlaid with veneers, deep alcoves, columns decorated with gilt spirals, and a huge staircase with the bannisters delicately filigreed in simulated wrought iron passing diagonally across the rear to sweep round to centre-stage, with inset beneath it a pipe organ and its horseshoe-shaped keyboard.

'The inspiration was not just extravagant Hollywood homes, but the great, opulent American movie houses of the 1920s,' said Napier, 'they were after all the palaces of Norma Desmond's era.' In spite of its huge weight and size it was designed to float airily up and down and forward and back, often with members of the cast on it, supported by towers on each side of the stage. In order to fulfil the need to be able to see the crowded New Year party at Artie's at the same time as the contrasting arid interior of Norma's house and its tango band playing endlessly to an empty floor, the set is lifted, and the young

JOHN NAPIER'S SET DESIGN: **ABOVE** 'THE HOUSE ON SUNSET', A HOME FOR A SILENT MEGASTAR; **TOP RIGHT** THE PARAMOUNT GATE; **BOTTOM RIGHT** THE MODEL OF THE *SAMSON AND DELILAH* SET; **FAR RIGHT** A FAMOUS FILM SHOT REPRODUCED ON STAGE – JOE'S BODY IN THE POOL

Napier was required to provide on stage the Paramount gate, a set for Cecil B DeMille's 1949 epic *Samson and Delilah* with the chaos and hubbub of a movie being made, the interior of Schwab's drug store, with its counters, newsstand and banquettes, Sheldrake's palatial art-deco office at the studio, and Betty's cramped working quarters in the writers' building, as well as the backlot at night with scenery representing New York

hopefuls fill the lower part of the stage, which becomes the cramped apartment's living room and the adjoining bathroom.

'The main problem dictating the way the set moves,' said Napier 'was the lack of backstage space. We have the stage trucks on each side, moving in and out, and that's all the wing space taken up. People have to clamber over them all night long. If we had put *Sunset Boulevard* on at Drury Lane we would have kept the set at the back and moved it downstage whenever we wanted. At the Adelphi we had to find another way of doing it, and that produced the split-screen effect. But I didn't want it to be seen as a high-tech show, nor as a fantasy, like *Cats*.'

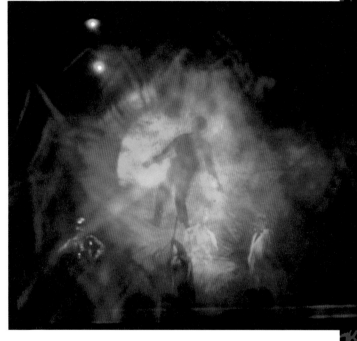

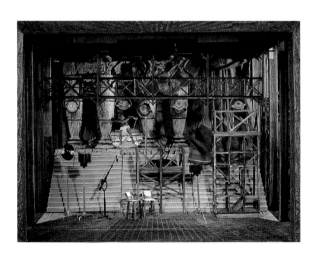

streets. One of the most challenging effects was a simulation of Wilder's famous view from below of the floating body in the swimming pool at the opening of the film, in which Joe Gillis is discovered floating face downwards with three bullet holes in him. The stage version uses a theatrical gauze canted at a forty-five degree angle to the stage, with the actor's body lying on it, and police and photographers discernible behind, the illusion of rippling water and dawn light created by the lighting. 'That particular effect was my first idea, before I had done any other work on *Sunset*,' said John Napier. 'When it came to the technical rehearsals it proved to be very difficult to get right, again because there's no backstage space to spare, and everything has to be in position precisely.'

One of the central features of Napier's design are a dozen dun-coloured sliders, which drop down in line in two groups of six, upstage and downstage, supplemented with two horizontal sliders to create openings. They are used to enable scene changes to go on behind them, and in themselves perform an integral scenic function, such as represent-

———— ◆ ————

BELOW SILHOUETTES ARE PROJECTED ON THE NEUTRAL-COLOURED SLIDERS, EVOKING SOUTHERN CALIFORNIAN ATMOSPHERE

ing the side of a Paramount soundstage. Silhouettes of palm trees, Norma Desmond's mansion, her ancient limousine and other cut-out images are occasionally projected on them to create a stage effect. While Napier borrowed ideas from the cinema, he was as anxious as Trevor Nunn that most of the solutions to staging problems should come from traditional theatrical methods. Projected sil-

ABOVE THE PARAMOUNT GATE ON STAGE

———— ◆ ————

houettes were often an element of Victorian melodrama. 'I very much wanted for it not to appear high-tech, for the audience not to be distracted by elaborate effects,' said Napier.

The sequence in the second act when Norma visits her old studio again for the first time in twenty years is a fine example of the designer's stagecraft. A replica of the famous Paramount gate faces the audience, and the car is heard approaching from stage left, its projected shadow visible. A gateman walks towards it and declines admission without a pass. Max then walks onto the stage as if he had just clambered from the chauffeur's seat, and remonstrates with him. Norma's voice is heard offstage addressing another, much older guard: 'Jonesy!' who looks up, instantly recognizes her (still invisible to the audience) and makes to open the gate as the sliders drop into position, becoming the side of the *Samson and Delilah* soundstage, its number projected onto it. Cecil B DeMille then enters from stage right with his surrounding aides, and is made aware that Norma Desmond has arrived. There is a greeting as she enters, and he motions to her to follow him onto the

ABOVE A CECIL B DEMILLE SOUND STAGE;
THE TEMPLE SCENE IN *SAMSON AND DELILAH*

stage, and as he does so the sliders are whisked away to reveal the frenzied movie set, alive with activity as the crew prepares for the next shot and the actor playing Samson flexes his biceps as he stands between the plaster columns of the temple ready to push them asunder. Norma is almost insignificant as she eases herself into DeMille's tall canvas chair, but above her on a lighting gantry an elderly electrician calls her with excitement, and swings a spotlight on her, whereupon everybody senses that someone

with a remarkable presence is there with them, and the costumed extras gather round, as she delivers the emotionally affecting song 'As If We Never Said Goodbye'.

The costume designs were the responsibility of Anthony Powell, a triple Oscar winner for *Tess*, *Death on the Nile* and *Travels With My Aunt*. His other film work includes two of Steven Spielberg's *Indiana Jones* films and *Hook*, and he has dressed the casts of many Royal Shakespeare and National Theatre productions. His experience in film provided invaluable references for recreating the Hollywood fashion look of 1949-50, particularly with regard to the young people swarming in Schwab's drugstore and attending Artie's party, attired in the casual styles of the period which to a modern eye look almost over-dressed. It was before the age of the ubiquitous blue denim; men tended to wear tan slacks, loose sports jackets and polo shirts open at the neck, and women usually wore skirts, sweaters, heels and patterned dresses. Busts were prominent, it was the era of the padded uplift bra. More formal clothes leaned towards full skirts and tight waists, and the

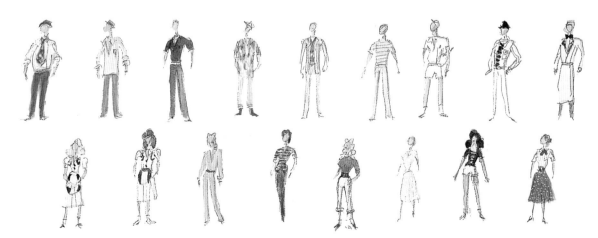

ABOVE COSTUME DESIGNER ANTHONY POWELL DREW HUNDREDS OF THUMBNAIL SKETCHES
TO SHOW THE CHANGES FOR EVERY CAST MEMBER

black silk suit and white boa worn by Norma on her visit to the studio is not far removed from Dior's fashion watershed, the 'New Look' of 1947. 'As far as ordinary street clothes are concerned it was not a very exciting period,' said Powell, 'too soon for the excesses of the Sixties. In 1950 the look was quiet and rather wholesome. But in California the clothes had more colour than elsewhere, and there was a very characteristic range of colour that I've gone for, a sort of bright Technicolor look.'

The costuming of Norma Desmond represented an exhilarating challenge for the designer. Her clothes had to be appropriate to a great star whose heyday is over, but at the same time appropriate to 1950 rather than 1925. Whatever illusions the character has on turning back the clock as far as her career is concerned, her dress sense was to be intact; bold, extravagant, luxurious, but not anachronistic, befitting a

star. Norma is never caught lounging around her vast house in anything less than a lamé housecoat and a gilt turban, although she might be seen at the poolside in a chic black and white striped robe. For her final moments she descends her grand staircase in a black cape trimmed with ostrich feathers, but by then the elaborate wig has gone, and the audience is very aware of her patchy white hair. 'Anthony Powell is wonderful – he inspired me,' said Patti LuPone. Their rapport was cemented when Powell journeyed to her remote home on the summit of a wooded Connecticut mountain during the spring thaw, and discussed her own dress tastes.

The costuming is an essential, sensitive element of the show. Joe, on the other hand, is initially clad in the sports jacket and baggy slacks of the era, a look that causes Norma to wince, and provides her with the excuse to tog him out to her own taste in 'The Lady's Paying' number. When Joe appears at Artie's party and doffs his hugely expensive vicuna overcoat, revealing that he's wearing an immaculate outfit of white tie and tails, he elicits from his host the remark 'Who did you borrow this from? Adolphe Menjou?' – a reference to an actor renowned for his suave sartorial presence.

Most modern film directors, rather than making conscious fashion statements as they work, prefer comfort, and attire themselves in garb as casual as tee-shirts and jeans, often rendering them indistinguishable from the humblest stagehands. In 1950 different standards still prevailed. On the set Cecil B DeMille almost always wore a well-cut hacking jacket and breeches with mirror-polished tan riding boots, an old-fashioned assertive touch appropriate to a veteran of the days of the pioneering silent pictures, and in the show he is portrayed by Michael Bauer in these characteristic working clothes. Similarly Max, also revealed later as a silent-movie director, wears a traditional butler's livery of black suit and butterfly-tipped collar, and when he is behind the wheel of the Isotta-Fraschini, a chauffeur's cap, high-buttoned tunic, breeches and black knee-length boots.

Before rehearsals on stage began a disturbing problem arose that threatened the future of the entire show. The set was so intricate that it was essential for the cast to get used to working on it, learning its movements, particularly for their own safety, since an actor in the wrong position could find himself in the way of several tons of descending scenery. It was found that parts of the set

would, without warning, move of their own accord. The mystery was eventually located to the electronics that controlled the hydraulic motors used for driving the sets, but the cause was elusive. Then engineers working beneath the stage discovered that when they used their portable telephones movements occurred. It was realized that the electronic valves in the hydraulic system were susceptible to signals from portable telephones, radio taxis, motorbike messengers and a myriad of other sources of interference. Vickers, the manufacturers of the equipment, were summoned and, conscious that a £3.5m investment was at stake, worked round the clock to find ways of screening out the unwanted signals. Said John Napier: 'Vickers had come up with a Mark II hydraulic valve, and everyone in the business was under the impression that it was a vast improvement on the old one.'

The only way to solve the problem was to strip out the Mark II valves and replace them with their predecessors, having first located a quantity sufficient to do the job. 'We lost ten days to two weeks because of it, and it meant also having to install bulky electronic units in the cramped area below the stage,' said Napier.

FAR LEFT PATTI LUPONE AS NORMA DESMOND, DRESSED TO KILL BY THE OSCAR-WINNING ANTHONY POWELL

LEFT ANTHONY POWELL'S THUMBLINE COSTUME SKETCHES

Because of the danger, the cast had been unable to rehearse on stage, and the date of the opening was approaching rapidly. The tight margin between the postponed start of stage rehearsals and the opening of the show, on 29 June, with previews due to begin on 21 June, had become untenable. Feeling acute disappointment for the cast and production staff Andrew Lloyd Webber was forced to

ABOVE ON STAGE FOR 'LET'S HAVE LUNCH'

announce the postponement of the first night to 12 July, with previews beginning on 28 June, thus gaining almost two extra weeks.

In itself a sensible and logical decision, the change caused a myriad of fresh problems. Booking for *Sunset Boulevard* had opened early in 1993 and a record box office advance had already been attained; by June all the seats for performances in the first weeks had been completely sold out. Advertisements were hastily inserted in the newspapers announcing the change, and offering those who found they had tickets for performances that were now previews the opportunity of an exchange for a later date or a full refund.

The biggest headache concerned the opening night itself, which was to be a celebrity-studded evening culminating in a huge party at The Savoy hotel, almost directly opposite the Adelphi. The Really Useful Theatre Company had to declare all tickets that had been sold void, and to issue new ones for other performances. It was an easy enough matter to trace ticket holders if they had paid by credit card, but many had been bought for cash at the box-office windows. There was a brief flurry of manufactured outrage in some sections of the press, who had prevailed upon disgruntled ticket holders to complain that they were being elbowed aside for free-loading first-nighters. Visions were conjured up of original purchasers turning up on the night of 12 July, waving their tickets and demanding to be seated, although Really Useful had the legal right to refuse admission. The company decided that should any people unaware of the postponement appear, a remote possibility given the huge publicity in the weeks prior to the opening, they would be offered a full refund, seats at another Lloyd Webber musical and tickets for *Sunset* at a later date. In the event it was unnecessary to dispense such largesse on the first night; in spite of the scares nobody with an old booking turned up.

The time gained by the postponement enabled the finishing touches to be put to the theatre. Napier had worked on the stage in some difficulty while building work had been going on in the rest of the theatre. 'We had 300 people there when we should only have had forty. The dust was terrible, and much of the place was a hard-hat area. That's not the best way to be installing sets.'

The dress rehearsal took place on the evening of Saturday, 26 June. Technical problems marred it, and the curtain was delayed for over an hour while efforts were made to free one of the two stage trucks which was supposed to wheel items of scenery such as the bedroom over the garage, the bathroom in Artie's apartment and the desk in the office in which Joe and Betty wrote their screenplay. Eventually it was decided to go ahead with the performance anyway and to have essential props carried on manually. It was a long evening, with an extra strain imposed on the cast by the scenic malfunction, and at the end Trevor Nunn resisted the urge to deliver his notes, and suggested that instead everybody should go home and get some sleep to be fresh for the first paid previews.

The custom of previewing big musicals is the modern equivalent of the out-of-town try-out, and because they take place in the same theatre in which the show will run, are a great deal more effective. The computer-controlled technical aspects of the production, the sets, lighting and sound, need a running-in period in order to find the weak points and to make corrections. 'The preview period is tremendously valuable,' said Trevor Nunn, 'to sense the audience response.' The reaction of a live audience enables reactions to be assessed, and lines can be sharpened or dropped, even scenes rewritten in time for the official opening. 'Changing a line isn't done instantly,' said Don Black. 'It has to be rehearsed first, and Trevor has to be satisfied. So if Chris and I make a change it would not usually be incorporated until two nights later. And if Andrew changes the score there's even more to do.'

Nevertheless, Andrew Lloyd Webber, Don Black and Christopher Hampton were in constant attendance, ready to make necessary adjustments. It was found, for instance, that the motive for Paramount calling Norma Desmond's home which she tragically misinterprets, namely that they wanted to borrow her car for a Bing Crosby picture, did not come across very clearly, being contained in a song. It was rewritten entirely as spoken dialogue, with Sheldrake, the producer seen in the first act, button-holing Max and crassly offering a hundred dollars a week for the use of the Isotta-Fraschini, so for the audience the point was made much more forcibly.

The finale, in which Norma becomes insane after killing Joe, and is persuaded by Max to descend the staircase to be taken into custody, needed special attention. An ostrich-feathered toque, towering three feet above her head drew too much attention, and disappeared after a few previews.

More fundamentally, there was a feeling that the ending did not work satisfactorily, and the initial audience response confirmed the feeling of anti-climax. Andrew Lloyd Webber felt that musically there had to be a big finish, not a slow fade. Norma's last speech had the famous line 'I'm ready for my close-up' buried within it, and ended with the words 'This is my life. It always will be. There is nothing else. Just us and the cameras and all you wonderful people out there in the dark.' It was, argued Hampton, a more logical connection to the audience sitting in the theatre. However, it also dispensed with one of the most celebrated last lines in movies, known widely even to those who had never actually seen the film, and its removal to a different place in the speech risked the possibility of generating unease at the most crucial moment of the performance, when the last impression of the show would be established.

During the weekend immediately preceding the first night of Monday 12 July the last scene was reshaped, with new musical sections and the crucial speech restored to its correct order. After an intensive session Lloyd Webber had achieved his big finish. The postponed opening night prolonged the publicity that *Sunset Boulevard* had constantly attracted. Magazines with long deadlines had already gone to press when the changed date was announced, and a flurry of articles had already appeared at the end of June. A steady stream of news and gossip on the show had been appearing ever since the workshop performance at Sydmonton and speculation over the casting in the previous September. In charge of press relations was Peter Thompson, a master in the craft of publicising London musicals, who had in a twenty-year career promoted productions by Michael White, Cameron Mackintosh and Andrew Lloyd Webber. 'I can't think of any other show that had so much pre-publicity as *Sunset*,' he said. 'There was never any let-up in media interest.'

Crowds gathered in the summer evening sunshine on the first night to watch the invited audience arrive, hampering the police's efforts to keep the traffic moving. In the midst of the black-tied assembly of stars and celebrities was Billy Wilder, accompanied by his wife, Audrey. Although the curtain rose a few minutes late the performance ran smoothly, and at the end, as the critics were racing out of the theatre Kevin Anderson and Patti LuPone were given standing ovations.

Nearly a thousand guests adjourned to The Savoy for the most lavish first-night party of the decade, with four of the hotel's huge public rooms commandeered for the occasion, and a menu that included Le Saumon Sunset, La Délice de Norma (breast of chicken on a bed of potato purée) and La Boîte de Chocolat Boulevard. Billy Wilder sat at the honoured place on Andrew Lloyd Webber's table, and expressed pleasure at the production. As each of the principals arrived they were cheered to their tables, Patti LuPone even jumping on hers to acknowledge the applause.

'What they have done is so clever,' commented Wilder on the staging, 'when you make a film you choose what shot to have, long, medium or close-up, you choose your lens, you have hundreds of ways to determine what the audience will see. On stage you cannot do that. Yet they have still managed to focus the attention where they wanted it to be focused. I wish I could do that.'

Also present was Nancy Olson, who played Betty Schaefer, and is now Mrs Alan Livingstone, wife of one of Los Angeles' most successful businessmen. She and Billy Wilder are the only survivors of the film. 'Watching the show tonight was like seeing my young life again,' she said. 'Simply remaking that film would have been pointless, but Andrew Lloyd Webber has enhanced it, moved it into a different domain. I can't wait to get home to California to look at the film all over again. Working on it was extraordinary for a young actress in Hollywood.'

During the party the first editions of the morning papers began to arrive. Two of them,

The Times and the *Guardian*, had broken tradition by printing their reviews on the front page, a measure of the importance with which the opening was regarded. Lloyd Webber shows have high news value, but are rarely regarded with unalloyed enthusiasm by theatre reviewers. It was not surprising therefore that the reviews were mixed, enthusiasm tempered with reservations on aspects of the performances and staging. On the day that *Sunset Boulevard* opened the closure of another musical set in Hollywood in the late-1940s, *City of Angels*, was announced, only four months into its run, and many of the critics referred to the coincidence in their notices. So much so that, given all the publicity stemming from *Sunset Boulevard*, audiences began to flock to *City of Angels* and its management took the unprecedented step of withdrawing the posted closure notice.

The consensus view of the London critics was that Lloyd Webber's show had the advantage of the familiarity of its story and the power of his music, which has managed to bring a sense of opera to the popular stage musical. Part of the ritual of a Lloyd Webber opening in New York is the traditional mauling by Frank Rich, the incumbent of the theatre review desk at *The New York Times*. Rich flew over to London, and managed to discern some praiseworthy aspects, particularly Kevin Anderson's performance, and the opening numbers of both acts with its 'surprisingly dark, jazz-accented music, the most interesting I've yet encountered from this composer.' Lloyd Webber has proved to be the most critic-proof of Rich's targets in a town where 'the butcher of Broadway' has sometimes succeeded in closing shows

instantly, the despondent managements seeing no point in carrying on. The public is the ultimate arbiter, and Lloyd Webber knows his public. Giving him particular pleasure was the re-assessment of the Master of the Queen's Music, the composer Malcolm Williamson who, earlier, had been dismissive of Lloyd Webber's work, describing it as 'factitious and repugnant'. After making a point of seeing *Sunset Boulevard* he completely changed his mind and in an interview with Rebecca Fowler in *The Sunday Times* compared it to Mozartian *singspiel*: 'It is technically marvellous. It also has spiritual and philosophical depth to it. This music is immortal.' Williamson, totally converted, continued: 'He has his finger on the pulse of something very

ABOVE NEW YEAR AT ARTIE'S, JOE IN BATHROOM

beautiful and only a composer of such technical skill could bring it off. It must be taken every bit as seriously as the most significant developments in opera from *The Magic Flute* to Benjamin Britten.' He added that the great composers were often insufficiently recognized by the critics, and that Bizet died heartbroken after the initial response to *Carmen*.

ABOVE LET'S HAVE LUNCH: THE OPENING ENSEMBLE NUMBER

RIGHT JOE IS HARRASSED BY THE REPOSSESSION MEN

LEFT LET'S HAVE LUNCH: JOE WITH ENSEMBLE

BELOW HOLLYWOOD HOPEFULS GO INTO THEIR DANCE

TOP SHELDRAKE AND BETTY DISCUSS
JOE'S SCREENPLAY

◆

ABOVE SHELDRAKE: A PRODUCER IN HIS MILIEU

◆

INSET RIGHT LAMENT FOR A DEAD FRIEND: A PET IS
PREPARED FOR BURIAL

◆

RIGHT NORMA MAKES A STARRY GESTURE

ABOVE JOE'S CAR IS HIDDEN IN NORMA'S GARAGE AS NIGHT FALLS

◆

BELOW NORMA UNTIES HER MANUSCRIPT RIBBON

◆

RIGHT JOE WADES THROUGH NORMA'S *SALOME*

RIGHT THE PROJECTOR CONCEALED IN A NICHE

BELOW DETAIL OF JOHN NAPIER'S SET OF THE DESMOND MANSION: INSPIRED BY AMERICAN PALACES OF DREAMS

A BRITISH INITIATIVE

LEFT 'NEW WAYS TO DREAM'

◆

BELOW NORMA AND JOE WATCH
HER SILENT MOVIE

ABOVE JOE MEETS
BETTY BY ARRANGEMENT
AT SCHWAB'S

◆

RIGHT ARTIE AND
JOE IN SCHWAB'S,
A SUNSET BOULEVARD
INSTITUTION

ABOVE NEW TOGS FOR JOE – 'THE LADY'S PAYING'

◆

RIGHT NEW YEAR'S EVE: NORMA KISSES HER
TANGO PARTNER

THE LONELY MANSION, THE CROWDED
APARTMENT ON NEW YEAR'S EVE

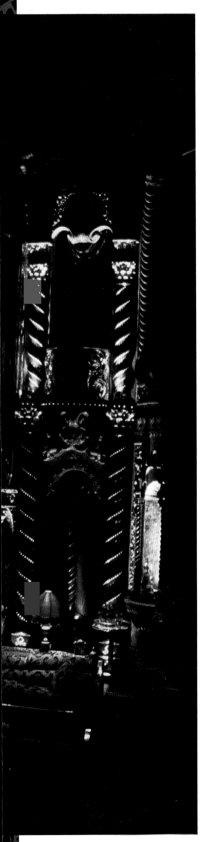

ABOVE THE LADY HAS SLASHED HER WRISTS

◆

LEFT JOE COMFORTS THE DISTRAUGHT NORMA

LEFT JOE BY NORMA'S POOL; NOW A KEPT MAN

BELOW THE PARAMOUNT GATE

ABOVE MAX TAKES
THE SCREENPLAY TO
PARAMOUNT

◆

RIGHT NORMA'S
CUT-DOWN MANUSCRIPT

A   B R I T I S H   I N I T I A T I V E

BELOW NORMA ON THE SET OF
SAMSON AND DELILAH

◆

BOTTOM JOE WITH BETTY IN HER OFFICE

◆

RIGHT NORMA TRANSFIXES CAST AND CREW
'WITH ONE LOOK'

LEFT MAX REPRISES
'NEW WAYS TO DREAM'

BELOW NORMA GETS
TONED UP FOR SALOME

ABOVE JOE AND BETTY SING THEIR
FALLING-IN-LOVE SONG

RIGHT NORMA MAKES A CALL WITH
MALICE, TO BETTY

A B R I T I S H I N I T I A T I V E

TOP JOE REVEALS TO BETTY WHAT HE REALLY IS

◆

LEFT NORMA BEGINS THE DESCENT INTO MADNESS

◆

ABOVE BETTY MEETS HER MATCH AND LOSES JOE

RIGHT THE FINAL
CONFRONTATION:
NORMA PLEADS
WITH JOE

ABOVE BETTY IS
UNABLE TO FACE JOE

RIGHT UNHINGED
NORMA SHOOTS HIM

RIGHT NORMA
PREPARES FOR HER
FINAL CLOSEUP

PART THREE

THE
LIBRETTO

CONTENTS

LOS ANGELES 1949/50

ACT ONE

ACT TWO

Entr'acte

ONE	Exterior	The House on Sunset	Day
		Sunset Boulevard – JOE	
		The Perfect Year (Reprise) – NORMA	
TWO	Exterior/	Paramount	Day
	Interior	**As If We Never Said Goodbye – NORMA**	
		Surrender (Reprise) – CECIL B DEMILLE	
THREE	Interior	Betty's Office	Night
		Girl Meets Boy (Reprise) – BETTY, JOE	
FOUR	Interior	The House on Sunset	Day
		Eternal Youth is Worth a Little Suffering – NORMA'S	
		CONSULTANTS	
FIVE	Interior/	Betty's Office/Paramount Backlot	Night
	Exterior	**Too Much in Love to Care – BETTY, JOE**	
SIX	Exterior	The House on Sunset	Night
		New Ways to Dream (Reprise) – MAX	
SEVEN	Interior/	The House on Sunset	Night
	Exterior	**Sunset Boulevard (Reprise) – JOE, BETTY**	
EIGHT	Exterior/	The House on Sunset	Dawn
	Interior	**The Greatest Star of All (Reprise) – MAX, NORMA**	

All bold type indicates sung lines.

The Libretto is published as performed at the world premiere on 12 July 1993; variations may occur during a performance.

Lyrics reproduced by kind permission of Don Black and Christopher Hampton.
Copyright © The Really Useful Group Ltd 1993

ACT ONE

ONE
.... THE HOUSE ON SUNSET ....

The patio and exterior of a preposterous, Italianate Hollywood mansion, not more than twenty years old, but already shabby from neglect. The deep end of the swimming pool is visible, the rest stretching off into the wings. Floating in the pool, fully clothed, face down, is the body of a young man. Dawn is just beginning to break.

Over this image, once it has become established, the VOICE of JOE GILLIS.

JOE (V.O.): **I guess it was five am.**
A homicide had been reported
from one of those crazy mansions
up on Sunset.
Tomorrow every front page
is going to lead with this story;
you see an old time movie star is involved
maybe the biggest star of all.

By now, a handsome, broad-shouldered man in his early thirties has emerged from the crowd and moved downstage to address the audience directly: this is JOE GILLIS.

JOE: **But before you read about it**
before it gets distorted
by those Hollywood piranhas
if you wanna know the real facts
you've come to the right party.

During this, the stage is irregularly raked by cold blue light which turns out to be thrown by the LAPD patrol cars, one of which draws up and disgorges a number of POLICEMEN, who split up; two approach the house, while another two move over to contemplate the body in the pool.

TWO
.... PARAMOUNT ....

The gates and open areas at the front of the Paramount lot, leading to the studios and the administration blocks. It is morning and a variety of young hopefuls are milling about in the forecourt, waiting for their interviews, assignments or auditions, and trying to impress one another. As this world gradually assembles before our eyes, JOE's tone changes; he continues to address the audience.

JOE (V.O.): **Let me take you back six months**
I was at the bottom of the barrel.
I'd had a contract down at Fox
but I'd fallen foul of Darryl.
Now I had a date at Paramount.
Along with about a thousand other writers,
If this didn't come up roses
I'd be covering funerals
back in Dayton, Ohio.
I'd hidden my car three blocks away
Turned out to be a smart move.

JOE approaches the gate, where he's challenged by JONES, the elderly guard. Underscoring continues.

JOE: Yeh, I've got an appointment with Mr Sheldrake.

JONES: Name?

JOE: Gillis. Joseph Gillis.

JONES consults his clipboard.

JONES: OK, sir, you know your way.

He waves JOE through and JOE joins the young hopefuls: these include MYRON, a director; MARY, a young actress, blonde and beautiful, artfully dishevelled; JOANNA, a writer, dark and intense; CLIFF, a cameraman; and KATHERINE, a willowy, pale New York actress. They weave in and out of the technicians shifting heavy equipment and the costumed extras, greeting each other with air-kisses, casual waves and ritualized exchanges.

JOE: Hi there, Myron.

MYRON: How's it hanging?

JOE: I've got a date with Sheldrake.

MYRON: I'm shooting a Western down at Fox.

JOE: How can you work with Darryl?

MYRON: We should talk.

JOE: Gotta run.

BOTH: Let's have lunch.

MARY: Hi, Mr Gillis.

JOE: You look great.

MARY: I'm up for an audition.

JOE: Sheldrake is driving me insane.

MARY: Don't forget me when you're casting.

JOE: We should talk.

MARY: Gotta run.

BOTH: Let's have lunch.

JOE: Morning Joanna.	**MARY:** Hi there, Myron.
JOANNA: Hi, how're you doing?	**MYRON:** How's it hanging?
JOE: I've got a date with Sheldrake.	**MARY:** I'm up for an audition.
JOANNA: I'm handing in my second draft.	**MYRON:** I'm shooting a Western down at Fox.
JOE: I'd really love to read it.	**MARY:** Don't forget me when you're casting.
JOANNA: We should talk.	**MYRON:** We should talk.
JOE: Gotta run.	**MARY:** Gotta run.
BOTH: Let's have lunch.	**BOTH:** Let's have lunch.

As he moves away from JOANNA, JOE is suddenly waylaid by two men in hats and bad suits: FINANCEMEN.

1ST FIN: We want the keys to your car.

2ND FIN: You're way behind with the payments.

1ST FIN: Don't give us any fancy footwork . . .

2ND FIN: Give us the keys.

JOE: I only wish I could help
I loaned it to my accountant.
He has an important client down in Palm Springs
Felt like playing some golf.

1ST FIN: Are you telling us you walked here?

JOE: I believe in self-denial.
I'm in training for the priesthood.

2ND FIN: OK, wise guy. Three hundred bucks.

1ST FIN: Or we're taking the car.

2ND FIN: We have a court order.

JOE: I love it when you talk dirty.

CLIFF: Hey, Joe!

He slips away from them, back into the social whirl. The FINANCEMEN meanwhile, by no means convinced, settle down to watch and wait.

JOANNA: Hi there, Mary.	**CLIFF:** Where've you been hiding?
MARY: How're you doing?	**JOE:** What are you shooting?
JOANNA: Writing for Betty Hutton.	**CLIFF:** I'm trying to make my mind up.
MARY: I'm up for something really big.	**JOE:** Why don't you ever call me back.
JOANNA: Should you undo a button?	**CLIFF:** Hey, isn't that your agent?
MARY: We should talk.	**JOE:** We should talk.
JOANNA: Gotta run.	**CLIFF:** Gotta run.
BOTH: Let's have lunch.	**BOTH:** Let's have lunch.

JOE moves swiftly towards a sharply-dressed middle-aged man, MORINO, his agent. MORINO is with a very much younger man and does his best to pretend not to notice JOE. When he realizes the encounter is unavoidable, he makes a great show of pleasurable surprise and greets JOE with effusive bonhomie.

MORINO: Greetings, Gillis.
What brings you here?

JOE: You're the one who fixed the date.

MORINO: Make it quick, don't keep us waiting.
We're with Sheldrake
10. 15.

JOE: Who is this?

MORINO: He's my new boy.

BOY: I have a play on Broadway.

MORINO: In verse. Every major studio is . . .

JOE *(interrupting)*: I need two hundred dollars.

MORINO *(to his boy)*: He's always been a joker.

JOE: OK, a hundred. I really need some money.

MORINO: Maybe what you need is a new agent.

He turns his back on JOE, puts his arm around his new boy and moves off, murmuring in his ear. JOE watches them for a second, then checks his watch and continues his progress through the constantly developing ballet of salutations. An instrumental section, during which a GRIP makes his way towards one of the studio buildings, carrying a step-ladder.

GRIP: What can I tell you? It's for Alan Ladd's
love-scene.

A group of extras from Cecil B DeMille's latest extravaganza 'Samson and Delilah' crosses the stage: JOE thinks he recognizes a man with a false beard and gold helmet who's accompanied by a gaggle of scantily-clad dancing girls: SAMMY. He raises his hand in a priestly gesture:

SAMMY: Bless you, Joseph.

JOE: That you, Sammy?

SAMMY: How do you like my harem?

JOE: How come you get such lousy breaks?

SAMMY: One learns to grin and bear 'em.

GIRLS: This is the
biggest film
ever made.

JOE: What're you playing?

1ST GIRL: Temple Virgin.

2ND GIRL: Handmaiden to Delilah.

JOE: Let's have lunch.

JOE spots another friend of his, ARTIE GREEN, a fresh-faced assistant director in his mid-twenties.

JOE: Hello, Artie.

ARTIE: Joe, you bastard!

JOE: You never call me any more.

ARTIE: Found a cuter dancing-partner.
How are things?

JOE: Not so great.

ARTIE: Will this help?

He hands JOE a twenty-dollar bill; JOE hesitates, then accepts it.

JOE: Thanks, you're a pal. I'll pay you back.

ARTIE: When you sign your contract.

JOE nods, pats ARTIE on the shoulder and moves on.

ALL: *(ad lib)* Good morning Mr De Mille.

JOE: I just love Hollywood.

The light hits JOE. Splintered lines overlap, creating a nightmarish cacophony of phoney greetings

MYRON: Morning, Joanna.

CLIFF: Where've you been hiding?

SAMMY: Hi there, Lisa.

MYRON: How're you doing?

KATHERINE: I hate this weather.

CLIFF: You look great.

LIZ: RKO are OK!

MARY: What're you doing?

JOANNA: You look great.

GIRLS: This is the biggest film ever made.

CLIFF: I'm trying to make my mind up.

MARY: Guess I was born to play her.

DAWN: What is my motivation?

JOANNA: You look great.

SAMMY: They're talking nominations.

LIZ: You should go work for Warners'.

MYRON: Is your new script with Sheldrake?

MORINO: I'm very close to Sheldrake

ARTIE: We shoot next month.

ADAM: (to Myron): I just signed.

SAMMY/SANDY/ARTIE/MORINO/MYRON: Gotta run.

JOHN: Let's drive to Vegas this weekend.

KATHERINE & JOANNA: Let's have lunch.

ANITA: You look great.

JOANNA: I'm handing in my second draft.

MARY: It's between me and Dietrich.

KATHERINE: I've landed a big Broadway show.

ADAM: I'm gonna work for Metro.

CLIFF: Let's have lunch.

MARY: Let's have lunch.

GIRLS: Let's have lunch, this is the biggest film ever made.

MYRON: I'd really love to read it.

CLIFF: I'd know just how to light you.

JOHN: Let's have lunch.

JOHN/LISA: It won't work.

MORINO: Let's pencil Thursday morning.

GROUP 1: We should talk.

GROUP 2: Gotta run.

CHORUS: Let's have lunch.

CHORUS: Hi, good morning, aren't we lucky?
    Going to work with Cukor.
    Paramount is paradise, movies from A to Zukor.
    We should talk, gotta run.

GROUP 1: Let's have lunch.

GROUP 2: We should talk.

GROUP 1: Gotta run.

GROUP 2: Gotta run.

ALL: Let's have lunch!

Meanwhile, the lights have come up on SHELDRAKE's office. SHELDRAKE, a mournful dyspeptic figure, sits behind a big desk, innocent of books, speaking into one of his array of 'phones.

GROUP 1: We should talk.

SHELDRAKE: This is Sheldrake . . .

GROUP 2: We should talk.

SHELDRAKE: Get me that shithead Nolan.

GROUP 1: Gotta run.

GROUP 2: Gotta run.

ALL: Let's have lunch!

Meanwhile, outside, the ceremony of empty greetings continues, occasionally interrupted by SHELDRAKE's harsh comments, or odd lines emerging from the contrapuntal melee.

SHELDRAKE: *(A total change of tone)* Nolan, sweetheart,
    great to talk,
    I read your script this morning.
    It won't work.

SECRETARY: Mr Gillis.

SHELDRAKE: It won't work.
    Who needs lunch?

SHELDRAKE is shaking some bicarb into a tumbler of water and stirring it as JOE is shown into his office. He looks up, surprised, and makes an unconvincing stab at conviviality.

SHELDRAKE: Joe! What the hell brings you here?

JOE: You wanted to see me.

SHELDRAKE: I did?

He thinks for a moment, frowning ferociously, and downs his medicine.

SHELDRAKE: Any idea what about?

JOE: I sent you an outline.

SHELDRAKE: You did? I never saw it. Nobody tells me anything.

JOE: 'Bases Loaded'. It's a baseball story.

SHELDRAKE: So pitch.

JOE: It's about a rookie shortstop that's batting 347. The kid was once mixed up in a hold-up. Now he's trying to go straight, only. . .

SHELDRAKE: Wait a minute, I think I have read this.

He presses a buzzer on the intercom on his desk.

SHELDRAKE: Can somebody bring in whatever we have on..

He looks up at JOE, hoping for guidance.

JOE: 'Bases Loaded'.

SHELDRAKE: . . . 'Bases Loaded'.

He puts down the receiver, turns his attention back to JOE.

SHELDRAKE: They tell the kid he has to throw the World Series, am I right?

JOE: They're pretty hot for it over at Twentieth.

SHELDRAKE: Good!

JOE: No, I don't trust Zanuck. Can you see Ty Power as a shortstop? You've got the best man for it right on the lot: Alan Ladd.

There's a knock and BETTY SCHAEFER steps into the room. She's a clean-cut, bright-looking girl in her twenties. She advances on SHELDRAKE, dropping a folder on his desk, not noticing JOE.

BETTY: Here's that 'Bases Loaded' material, Mr Sheldrake. I made a two-page synopsis of it for you. But I wouldn't bother to read it.

SHELDRAKE: Why not?

BETTY: It's just a rehash of something that wasn't very good to begin with.

SHELDRAKE: Meet Mr Gillis. He wrote it.

BETTY turns to JOE, horribly embarrassed.

SHELDRAKE: This is Miss Kramer.

BETTY: Schaefer. Betty Schaefer. And right now, I'd like to crawl into a hole and pull it in after me.

JOE: If I could be of any help . . .

BETTY: I'm sorry, Mr Gillis, I couldn't see the point of it. I think pictures should at least try to say a little something.

JOE: I see you're one of the message kids. I expect you'd have turned down 'Gone with the Wind'.

SHELDRAKE: No, that was me.

BETTY: And I guess I was disappointed. I've read some of the stories you wrote for the magazines and I thought you had some real talent.

JOE: That was last year. This year I felt like eating.

BETTY: Well, I'm sorry, Mr Gillis.

JOE: Next time I'll write you 'The Naked and the Dead'.

SHELDRAKE: That'll be all, Miss Kramer.

BETTY leaves the room. SHELDRAKE looks up at JOE.

SHELDRAKE: Looks like Zanuck's got himself a baseball picture.

JOE: Have you got any kind of work?

SHELDRAKE: There's nothing. Unless . . . we're always looking for a Betty Hutton script. What if we made it a girl softball team? Put in a few numbers. Might make a cute musical.

JOE: Are you trying to be funny? Because I'm all out of laughs. I'm over a barrel. I need a job. Additional dialogue. Anything.

SHELDRAKE: Something may come up. I'll keep you in mind.

JOE: Listen, Mr Sheldrake, could you give me three hundred dollars? As a personal loan?

SHELDRAKE is dreadfully taken aback.

JOE: I've been grinding out original stories, two a week, for months now. Maybe they're not original enough. Maybe they're too original.

SHELDRAKE: The finest things in the world have been written on an empty stomach.

JOE: It's not my stomach I'm worried about, it's my car. If I lose that in this town, it's like having my legs cut off.

The 'phone rings and SHELDRAKE jumps at the opportunity to take the call. He turns back to JOE.

SHELDRAKE: Gillis, last year somebody talked me into buying a ranch in the valley, so I borrowed the money from the bank . . .

Back to the 'phone.

SHELDRAKE: Yes, OK, put him on.

Back to JOE.

SHELDRAKE: And this year I had to mortgage the ranch so I could keep up my life insurance payments . . .

He turns back to the 'phone; JOE gives up and walks out on him.

SHELDRAKE: He wants to see who? Brando? Brando? Take it from me, nobody wants to see that kid.

He turns back to continue his spiel, but JOE has vanished. JOE moves slowly, aware that the FINANCE MEN are waiting to intercept him. BETTY SCHAEFER is hurrying after him. The MUSIC starts up again, underscoring the dialogue.

JOE: Come to get your knife back? It's still here, right between my shoulder blades.

BETTY: You wrote a story, a couple of years back. About a teacher. Title something to do with windows.

JOE: 'Blind Windows'.

BETTY: I really liked it.

JOE: You're making me feel all warm and runny inside.

BETTY: Maybe I can get Sheldrake to option it.

Silence. JOE glances at the FINANCE MEN, circling like sharks.

JOE: I doubt it. He likes pictures with great weather and happy endings.

BETTY: Why don't you let me try?

JOE considers for a moment, tempted, hesitating.

BETTY: Let's get together.

JOE: That's what they all say.

BETTY: I'll be at Schwab's on Thursday
I'm always there round six o'clock.

JOE: I gotta check my diary.

BETTY: We should talk.

JOE: Gotta run.

BETTY: What's the rush?

He runs into an empty sound stage. She follows.

JOE: See those gorillas?

BETTY: Yes, what about them?

JOE: Do me a terrific favour.
Keep them amused while I escape.

BETTY: If you'll agree to Thursday.

JOE hesitates fractionally.

JOE: Done.

2ND FIN: There he is.

1ST FIN: Come 'n show us
Where you parked it.

2ND FIN: Or I'll reshape your face.

BETTY: Shhh! Please be quiet, Mr DeMille is shooting
through there.

1ST FIN: So what?

BETTY: He's working on one of Hedy's red hot scenes in
'Samson and Delilah'. Say . . . do you boys wanna go on the
set?

1ST FIN: No.

2ND FIN: (*Interrupting*) I think we maybe have five minutes.

*She leads him through a tall doorway and ingeniously
vanishes, leaving them disorientated for a moment. Then they
simultaneously realize they've been tricked and set off back
towards their car at a run.*

THREE
. . . . O N   T H E   R O A D . . . .

*JOE's car noses into one of the main boulevards near
Paramount; but the FINANCE MEN come roaring up in pursuit.
JOE hits the gas and a high speed chase ensues. Finally after a
hair-raising dash through the Holmby Hills, JOE's car turns on
to Sunset, gains some distance with an enterprising U-turn
and then suffers a sudden blow-out. With some difficulty, JOE
manages to control the car and turns into an open driveway,
which then curves away from the street, so that the FINANCE
MEN thunder by without seeing JOE's car.*

FOUR
. . . THE HOUSE ON SUNSET . . .

*The property is noticeably shabbier and more run
down than it was in the opening scene. The patio and little
formal garden are choked with weeds, the plants on the
balcony are overgrown and out of control and the pool is
covered over. JOE jumps out of his car.*

JOE: What a lovely sight: a great big empty garage.

*He pushes his car the last few yards into an open
garage: and discovers it is not empty after all. Under a
tarpaulin, which JOE lifts, curious, is the rear of an insanely
elaborate 1932 Isotta-Fraschini with speaking tubes, running-
boards, glass partitions and leopard-skin upholstery. He
contemplates it for a moment.*

JOE: This thing must burn up ten gallons to a mile.

*Then he emerges from the garage and starts walking
towards the house, as a ghostly version of 'New Ways to
Dream' begins. He comes to a halt, marvelling both at the
scale and the dereliction of the house.*

JOE: There had to be a house around here someplace, but the
garden was so neglected and overgrown, I couldn't for a
moment figure out where it was. At the same time, I felt cold
all of a sudden, you know, as if someone was walking over my
grave.

**Christ, where am I?
I had landed
in the driveway of some palazzo
like an abandoned movie set.**

*Suddenly he is startled by a sharp, decisive woman's
voice, cutting harshly into his reverie . . . .He looks up at the
balcony above but no one is visible.*

VOICE: You there!

*JOE approaches still searching in vain for the source of
the voice.*

VOICE: Why are you so late?

*Before he can summon up an answer, another shock;
the French doors grind open and an extraordinary figure
emerges from the house. This is MAX VON MAYERLING, a sixty-
year-old butler in black tail coat, striped trousers, stiff-collar
shirt and white cotton gloves. He contemplates JOE, his
expression blank; then speaks in some mitteleuropaisch accent.*

MAX: This way.

*JOE steps forward, responding to MAX's natural
authority.*

MAX: And wipe your feet!

JOE obeys and steps through the French doors.

The huge gloomy drawing room is revealed. The floor is tiled and the ceiling supported with dark heavy beams. There are framed photographs everywhere and musty hangings. The breeze moans through the pipes of a built-in organ. At the back of the room, on a massage table, something is lying, shrouded in a Spanish shawl, with candles in silver candlesticks burning at each corner of the table. The VOICE rings out again from above, where a black marble staircase, leads up to a broad gallery.

VOICE: Max! Tell him to wait!

MAX turns to JOE, his tone chilly.

MAX: You heard.

He starts to move off.

MAX: If you need my help with the coffin, call me.

JOE: Wait a minute . . . hey, Buddy . . .

But MAX is gone. JOE looks around, somewhat at a loss. But before he can make a move, the door to the gallery opens and another bizarre figure appears: NORMA DESMOND. Despite the gloom, she's wearing dark glasses and she's dressed in black loose pyjamas and black high heel pumps. She looks younger than her age, which is probably somewhere in the vicinity of fifty, and, despite a sickly pallor, she's extremely striking and was evidently once a great beauty. Her hair is encased in a leopard-patterned chiffon scarf. JOE watches her, transfixed, as she proceeds in stately fashion down the stairs.

NORMA: Any laws against burying him in the garden?

JOE: I wouldn't know.

NORMA: I don't care anyway.

She sweeps past him to the back of the room, where she stands for a moment looking down at the child-sized bundle on the massage table. JOE, all his writer's instincts now alerted, watches her, fascinated. The MUSIC swells.

NORMA: No more wars to fight
    white flags fly tonight
    you are out of danger now
    battlefield is still
    wild poppies on the hill
    peace can only come when you surrender.

    Here the tracers fly
    lighting up the sky
    but I'll fight on to the end
    let them send their armies
    I will never bend
    I won't see you now till I surrender
    I'll see you again when I surrender.

As the last echoes of this die away, she sweeps up the corpse into her arms, the shawl falls away and for the first time, we see the body is that of a chimpanzee. NORMA stares defiantly at JOE, the monkey's face cradled against her own.

NORMA: Now don't you give me a fancy price just because I'm rich.

JOE: Lady, you've got the wrong man.

NORMA pauses in the act of rearranging the corpse and shoots JOE a fierce glance.

JOE: I had some trouble with my car, I just pulled into your driveway.

NORMA: Get out.

JOE: OK. And I'm sorry you lost your friend.

NORMA: Get out of here.

JOE's almost out: then he turns back, frowning.

JOE: Haven't I seen you somewhere before?

NORMA: Or shall I call my servant?

JOE: Aren't you Norma Desmond? You used to be in pictures. You used to be big.

NORMA: I am big. It's the pictures that got small.

She advances on him, flushed with indignation.

NORMA: There was a time in this business
    you wouldn't remember
    we had the eyes of the whole wide world
    but that wasn't good enough
    for those Einsteins in the front office
    they wanted the ears of the world as well.

    So they took all the idols and smashed them.
    The Fairbanks, the Gilberts, the Valentinos
    they trampled on what was divine
    they threw away the gold of silence
    when all they needed was this face of mine.

JOE: Don't blame me, I'm just a writer.

JOE's back in the room now; watching as NORMA summons up before him the essence of her vanished stardom.

NORMA: With one look
    I can break your heart
    with one look
    I play every part
    I can make your sad heart sing
    with one look you'll know
    all you need to know.

    With one smile
    I'm the girl next door
    or the love that you've hungered for
    when I speak it's with my soul
    I can play any role.

    No words can tell
    the stories my eyes tell
    watch me when I frown
    you can't write that down
    you know I'm right
    it's there in black and white
    when I look your way
    you'll hear what I say.

    Yes, with one look
    I put words to shame
    just one look
    sets the screen aflame
    silent music starts to play
    one tear in my eye
    makes the whole world cry.

    With one look
    they'll forgive the past
    they'll rejoice: I've returned at last
    to my people in the dark
    still out there in the dark . . .

She sweeps majestically around the stage as the orchestra takes the melody.

NORMA: Silent music starts to play
With one look you'll know
all you need to know.

With one look
I'll ignite a blaze
I'll return to my glory days
they'll say Norma's back at last.

This time I am staying
I'm staying for good
I'll be back
where I was born to be
with one look
I'll be me.

She comes to herself suddenly, aware once again of his presence.

NORMA: Now go.

JOE: Next time I'll bring my autograph book or maybe a hunk of cement and ask for your footprint.

JOE nods good-naturedly, turns and sets off towards the French doors. He's almost out of them, when NORMA speaks again.

NORMA: Just a minute.

JOE stops in the doorway, half-turns back.

NORMA: Did you say you were a writer?

JOE: That's what it says on my guild card.

NORMA: And you've written pictures?

JOE: Sure have. Would you like to see my credits?

NORMA: Come over here, I want to ask you something.

JOE hesitates; but his curiosity gets the better of him and he begins to move back into the body of the room.

NORMA: What sort of length is a movie script these days?

JOE: Depends.

Standing by the sofa, next to the gold grand piano covered in photographs, is an immense manuscript, several bundles, each wrapped in red ribbon, standing about two feet high.

NORMA: I wrote this. It's a very important picture.

JOE: Looks like six very important pictures.

NORMA: It's for DeMille to direct.

JOE: Oh, yeah? And will you be in it?

NORMA: Of course. What do you think?

JOE: Just asking. I didn't know you were planning a comeback.

NORMA: I hate that word. It's a return.

JOE: Well . . . fair enough.

NORMA: I want you to read it.

This takes JOE by surprise; it takes him a moment to devise a response.

JOE: You shouldn't let another writer read your stuff. He may steal it.

NORMA: I'm not afraid. Sit down. Max!

JOE still dithers; MAX appears at once.

NORMA: Bring something to drink.

MAX: Yes, Madame.

JOE brightens; but still hesitates.

NORMA: I said sit down!

JOE lapses on to the sofa. The following sequence telescopes the passing of time covered by the reading of the script; but for now, NORMA, with great care, picks up the first of the bundles of manuscript, almost sensually slips off the ribbon and proffers it to JOE.

NORMA: It's about Salome.

MAX arrives wheeling a silver trolley, with champagne, caviar and red Venetian glasses. JOE takes the manuscript from NORMA and settles himself.

NORMA: Salome: the story of a woman. The woman who was all women.

He begins to read. MAX withdraws. NORMA hovers, watching JOE.

NORMA: Salome, what a woman, what a part!
Innocent body and a sinful heart,
inflaming Herod's lust,
but secretly loving a holy man.
No one could play her like I can.

She's off in a world of her own; so much so, that JOE is able to sing his lines directly to the audience, as he shifts through the pages and sips his champagne.

JOE: Well, I had nothing urgent coming up,
I thought I might as well skim it.
It's fun to see how bad bad writing can be,
this promised to go the limit.

NORMA paces impatiently: the light is beginning to fade.

NORMA: There's so many great scenes, I can't wait.
A boiling cauldron of love and hate.
She toys with Herod
till he's putty in her hands
he reels tormented through the desert sands.

MAX reappears and moves around the room, lighting lamps. JOE picks up another bundle.

JOE: It sure was a real cheery set-up,
the wind wheezing through that organ.
Max shuffling round and a dead ape dumped on a
    shelf
and her staring like a gorgon.

NORMA is on the stairs now, peering across the room at JOE.

NORMA: They drag the Baptist up from the jails.
    She dances the dance of the seven veils.

NORMA throws herself into an extravagant dance, distracting JOE.

NORMA: Herod says: 'I'll give you anything.'

JOE resumes reading as MAX shows in a man dressed in formal evening clothes: the PET UNDERTAKER. He has a baby coffin under his arm.

JOE: Now it was time for some comedy relief,
    the guy with the baby casket.
    Must have seen a thing or two, that chimp,
    shame it was too late to ask it.

During this, MAX and NORMA have followed the UNDERTAKER out into the garden, he having stowed the chimp in the coffin, wrapped in NORMA's shawl. Now NORMA reappears suddenly, startling JOE.

NORMA: Have you got to the scene where she asks for
        his head?
    If she can't have him living, she'll take him dead.
    They bring in his head on a silver tray.
    She kisses his mouth. It's a great
        screenplay!

JOE's on the last bundle now: NORMA lights herself a Turkish cigarette, having first inserted it in a holder attached to a curious clip which twists around her index finger.

JOE: It got to be eleven, I was feeling ill.
    What the hell was I doing?
    Melodrama and sweet champagne
    and a garbled plot from a scrambled brain;
    but I had my own plot brewing.

He lays down the last page with a slight sigh. NORMA is instantly alert.

JOE: Just how old is Salome?

NORMA doesn't bat an eyelid.

NORMA: Sixteen.

JOE: I see.

NORMA: Well?

JOE: It's fascinating.

NORMA: Of course it is.

JOE looks up at her, choosing his words judiciously.

JOE: Could be it's a little long
    maybe the opening's wrong
    but it's extremely good for a beginner.

NORMA: No it's a perfect start,
    I wrote that with my heart
    the River Bank, the Baptist and the Sinner.

JOE: Shouldn't there be some dialogue?

NORMA: I can say what I want with my eyes.

JOE: It could use a few cuts.

NORMA: I will not have it butchered!

JOE: I'm not talking limb from limb,
    I just mean a little trim
    all you need is someone who can edit.

NORMA: I want someone with a knack
    not just any studio hack
    and don't think for a moment I'd share credit!

NORMA stares at him, an idea beginning to form in her mind.

NORMA: When were you born?

JOE: December twenty-first, why?

NORMA: I like Sagittarians. You can trust them.

JOE: Thanks.

She turns on him, her eyes blazing.

NORMA: I want *you* to do this work.

JOE feigns a moment of surprise: then his eyes narrow and his voice is shrewd.

JOE: Me? Gee, I don't know, I'm busy. I just finished one script and about to start a new assignment

NORMA: I don't care.

JOE: I'm pretty expensive. I get five hundred a week.

NORMA: Don't you worry about money. I'll make it worth your while.

JOE is still not giving anything away. He pretends to reflect.

JOE: Well. It's getting kind of late.

NORMA: Are you married, Mr . . .?

JOE: The name is Gillis. Single.

NORMA: Where do you live?

JOE: Hollywood. Alto Nido Apartments.

NORMA: You'll stay here.

JOE: I'll come back early tomorrow.

NORMA: Nonsense, there's a room over the garage. Max will take you there. Max!

Rather unnervingly, MAX emerges from the shadows: he's been there for some time.

MAX: Yes, Madame.

NORMA: Take Mr Gillis to the guest room.

After a second's hesitation, JOE finds himself following MAX towards the French doors.

NORMA: We'll begin at nine sharp.

MAX, holding up a lamp, leads JOE across the dark patio and up an outside wooden staircase to an austere, small room above the garage.

JOE: Now this is more like it.

MAX: I made the bed up this afternoon.

JOE: Thanks.

He considers this for a moment.

JOE: How did you know I was going to stay?

MAX: There's soap and a toothbrush in the bathroom.

JOE: She's quite a character, isn't she, that Norma Desmond?

MAX is slightly scandalized by this remark; but he preserves his dignity and looks JOE straight in the eye.

MAX: [She is much more than that.] (*Optional*) Once,
you won't remember,
if you said Hollywood hers was the face you'd
   think of.
Her face on every billboard,
in just a single week she'd get ten
   thousand letters.

Men would offer
fortunes for a bloom from her corsage
or a few strands from her hair.

Today
she's half-forgotten,
but it's the pictures that got small.
She is the greatest star of all.

Then,
you can't imagine,
the way fans sacrificed themselves to touch her
   shadow.

There was
a maharajah
who hanged himself with one of her
   discarded stockings.

She's immortal,
caught inside that flickering light beam
is a youth which cannot fade.

Madame's
a living legend;
I've seen so many idols fall.
She is the greatest star of all.

He leaves the room. JOE watches him go, strangely impressed. Left alone, JOE moves restlessly around the room for a moment.

JOE (V.O.): When he'd gone, I stood looking out of the window a while. There was the ghost of a tennis court with faded markings and a sagging net. There was an empty pool where Clara Bow and Fatty Arbuckle must have swum 10,000 midnights ago. And then there was something else: the chimp's last rites, as if she were laying a child to rest. Was her life really as empty as that?

Below, MAX disappears for a moment into the shadow of the garage. Then, he re-emerges. He's carrying a shovel and, under his arm, the chimpanzee's coffin. He advances to a spot where there's an overgrown rosebed in the centre of the patio outside the French doors. As he arrives there, NORMA who's evidently been waiting, emerges into the garden. They stand for a moment in silent communion, the atmosphere solemn. Then MAX takes up the shovel.

Above in his room, JOE is about to pull the curtain when he catches sight of MAX and NORMA. He stands at the window, staring down at them, riveted by the peculiarity of the scene, shaking his head wonderingly.

SLOW FADE TO BLACK

F I V E
. . . . S C H W A B ' S   D R U G S T O R E . . . .

Schwab's is a Sunset Boulevard institution, a combination soda-fountain, newsstand, tobacconists and diner: it's crowded with movie people of one sort and another; including some we recognize from the opening scene at Paramount, MARY, for example, whose day-job is as a waitress at Schwab's (like Lana Turner); MYRON, the director; JOANNA, the writer; and ARTIE GREEN. BETTY sits in a booth, on her own, with her back to the door.

JOANNA: He says my screenplay's much too dark.

KATHERINE: What do they know, those morons.

JOHN: What's with you?

LISA: Some yes man
just said no.

ALISA: Hold the fries.

MARY: He asked me to screen test on my knees.

MYRON: He's always been religious.

SAMMY: Who's your agent?

LORNA: Marty Resnick.

SAMMY: Thought he went out of business.

ANITA: Bring the check.

ALISA: Ham on rye.

MARY: Cherry pie.

ANITA: What are you playing?

STEVE: Third policeman.

ANITA: Wonderful. Great. Fantastic.

SANDY: Where's your husband?

SASHA: He's in Reno.

GERARD: So are you free for dinner?

ADAM: Time to go.

SASHA: What's the rush?

SODA JERK: Two large shakes.

RICHARD: Six broiled dogs.

During this last round, JOE has entered the drugstore. He hesitates in the doorway, slightly disorientated by the hubbub and bustle after the sepulchral calm of NORMA'S house. ARTIE spots him and hurries over.

ARTIE: Joe, you bastard.
What brings you here?

JOE: I'm taking a creative note
from some snotty studio smartass.
What's with you?

ARTIE: I'm in love.

JOE: What, again?

ARTIE: No, no, no,
this is it.
The real thing.
Never thought it could happen like this,
saw myself as the Jewish Casanova,
but as soon as we shared our first kiss
I knew all my romancing days were over

now I'm up in the clouds and I'm head over heels.
I know it sounds corny,
but that's how it feels.

JOE: Great. Any chance of meeting this paragon?

ARTIE: Sure, just for a minute: she's due to have a meeting with some poor struggling hack.

He's steered JOE over to BETTY'S booth: when she sees him, she rises to her feet.

BETTY: Hello, Mr Gillis.

ARTIE: You two know each other?

JOE: Yeah, I'm the hack.

ARTIE: Oh, I'm sorry. And she's the smartass?

BETTY: Just a minute, you're leaving me way behind here.

JOE: Don't worry, we'd better have our meeting, I don't want to come between you two lovebirds a minute longer than I have to. Oh, and congratulations. May I?

He sits at the table next to BETTY, pointing up at ARTIE.

JOE: He tells me you've made a new man of him.

He turns to ARTIE.

JOE: And you've done real well, I'd say. Of course, she could use a little guidance in the literary appreciation department.

BETTY: I like 'Blind Windows'.

JOE: That's why I'm here.

BETTY: So have you had any ideas about how you could turn it into a movie?

JOE hesitates a moment; then settles back in his seat.

JOE: Girl meets boy.
That's a safe beginning.

ARTIE: Is this a Western?
I love those wide rolling plains.

BETTY: No it's not. They live in the city.

ARTIE: Then it's a thriller:
the sidewalk gleams when it rains.

Or how about a brilliant pianist?
Every time the full moon's on the rise
he can't play without a shot of virgin's blood.

BETTY: Thanks a lot.
Be sure to leave your number.

ARTIE: You'll think of something.
I'll see you opening night.

He moves off to join MYRON and JOANNA at another table. BETTY turns to JOE.

BETTY: Girl meets boy,
now if I remember
she's a young teacher,
he's a reporter
it's hate at first sight.

JOE: It won't sell,
these days they want glamour:
fabulous heiress
meets handsome Hollywood heel.
Problem is,
she thinks he's a dentist.
Would you believe it?
A wedding in the last reel.

BETTY: It doesn't have to be so mindless.
You should write from your experience
give us something really moving;
something true.

JOE: Who wants true?
Who the hell wants moving?
Moving means starving
and true means holes in your shoe.

BETTY: No, you're wrong.
They still make good pictures.
Stick to your story,
It's a good story.

JOE: OK, Miss Schaefer:
I give it to you.

He's on his feet; BETTY is looking up at him, completely wrong-footed by his unexpected reaction.

BETTY: What do you mean?

JOE: What I say. It's all yours. I've given up writing myself. So you write it.

BETTY: I'm not good enough to do it on my own. I thought we could write it together.

JOE: I can't. I'm all tied up.

BETTY: Couldn't we work evenings? Six o'clock in the morning? I'll come to your place.

JOE: Look, Betty, it can't be done. It's out.

He relents a little at her obvious disappointment, smiles apologetically.

JOE: Let's keep in touch through Artie. That way if you get stuck, we can at least talk. I've always been very liberal with advice.

He smiles down at her, relaxed now.

JOE: Write this down
I'll give you some ground rules
plenty of conflict
but nice guys don't break the law.
Girl meets boy
give herself completely
and though she loves him
she keeps one foot on the floor.

BETTY: No one dies except the best friend
no one ever mentions communists
no one takes a black friend to a restaurant.

JOE: Very good.
Nothing I can teach you
we could have had fun
fighting the studio.

BETTY: Yes, Mr Gillis,
that's just what I want.

They shake hands; the handshake lasts a little longer than strictly necessary and is interrupted indeed by the arrival of ARTIE.

ARTIE: Not going, are you? Come to the movies with us.

JOE: No, I was just explaining to Betty, I've given up the movies.

ARTIE: Well, will we see you New Year's Eve, my place, same as ever?

JOE: Yeh, sure, as long as you promise there'll be a lot of bad behaviour.

ARTIE: Guaranteed the worst in town.

JOE inclines his head to BETTY.

JOE: Miss Schaefer.

BETTY: Mr Gillis.

JOE: Good luck.

He turns and hurries out of the place.

S I X
T H E   H O U S E   O N   S U N S E T
. . . . (E X T E R I O R) . . . .

The house, ghostly in the moonlight. To begin with, the stage is empty; then JOE appears, moving silently across the patio. At a certain point he's startled, as MAX glides out through the French doors to intercept him.

MAX: Where have you been?

JOE: Out. I assume I can go out when I feel like it.

MAX: Madame is quite agitated. Earlier this evening, she wanted you for something and you could not be found.

JOE: Well, that's tough.

MAX: I don't think you understand, Mr Gillis. Madame is extremely fragile. She has moments of melancholy.

JOE: Why? Because of her career? She's done well enough. Look at all the fan mail she gets every day.

MAX: I wouldn't look too closely at the postmarks if I were you.

JOE: You mean you send them?

MAX: Will you be requiring some supper this evening, sir?

JOE: No. And Max?

MAX: Yes, sir?

JOE: Who the hell do you think you are, bringing my stuff over from my apartment without consulting me? I have a life of my own – now you're telling me I'm supposed to be a prisoner here.

MAX considers him for a moment, his eye cold.

MAX: I think, sir, perhaps you will have to make up your mind to abide by the rules of this house. That is if you want this job.

He turns: the house swallows him up and he disappears as abruptly as he materialized. JOE stands for a moment, perplexed: then he proceeds on his way up the wooden staircase towards his room above the garage.

S E V E N
T H E   H O U S E   O N   S U N S E T
. . . . (I N T E R I O R) . . . .

A table has been cleared for JOE in the main room. He sits at the typewriter, the manuscript piled at his elbow, a pencil held between his teeth, scissors and a pot of paste to hand. NORMA prowls the room, watching him avidly.

Over this, JOE's VOICE.

JOE (V.O.): I started work on the script,
I hacked my way through the thicket,
a maze of fragmented ramblings
by a soul in limbo.
She hovered there like a hawk,
afraid I'd damage her baby.

The house was always so quiet.
Just me and Max and the organ.
No one phoned and nobody ever came.
I couldn't breathe in that room
it was so full of Norma Desmond
and there was only one kind of
entertainment on hand.

During this MAX has been busying himself, setting up a projector and lacing up the reels. JOE wanders over to take his place on the sofa. Eventually, NORMA sweeps in, dressed to the nines and settles down next to JOE. MAX switches on the projector and the beam radiates out across the auditorium. For a while, the whirr of the projector; NORMA watches, looking out into the audience, entranced; while JOE, far more detached, lights himself a cigarette, the smoke drifting across the light-beam.

NORMA: This was dawn:
there were no rules,
we were so young.
Movies were born;
so many songs
yet to be sung.
So many roads
still unexplored;
we gave the world
new ways to dream.
Somehow we found
new ways to dream.

She takes JOE's arm excitedly and points up at the screen, somewhere above the audience's heads.

NORMA: Joan of Arc:
look at my face,
isn't it strong?
There in the dark.
Up on the screen,
where I belong.
We'll show them all
nothing has changed.
We'll give the world
new ways to dream.
Everyone needs
new ways to dream.

('With One Look' returns as underscoring.)

By now, she's gripping on to JOE, who detaches himself gently and moves to the other end of the sofa, where he turns to contemplate NORMA, who's still staring ecstatically at the screen.

JOE (V.O.): I didn't argue,
why hurt her?
You don't yell at a sleepwalker
or she could fall and break her neck.
She smelled of faded roses.
It made me sad to watch her
as she relived her glory.
Poor Norma,
so happy,
lost in her silver heaven.

NORMA continues to watch; and JOE watches her.

NORMA: They can't see where the future lies.
They don't recognize a star.

JOE is touched; he reaches out and takes her hand.

F A D E   T O   B L A C K

E I G H T

. . . . T H E   H O U S E   O N   S U N S E T . . . .

*The sound of heavy rain. It's daytime but dull enough
to need the lights on. JOE's typewriter is no longer on the
table, but closed and standing on end on the floor. He's alone
in the great room, playing solitaire. MAX is at the organ
wearing his white gloves, playing. JOE looks up at the
audience, breaks off from his game.*

JOE: In December, the rains came in one great package,
oversized, like everything else in California; it came right
through the roof of my room above the garage. So she had me
moved to the main house, to what Max called 'the room of the
husbands'. On a clear day, the theory was, you could see
Catalina. And little by little I worked through to the end of the
script. At which point I might have left: only by then those two
boys from the finance company had traced my car and towed
it away.

*He resumes his game: all of a sudden NORMA sweeps
out of her room and down the stairs; she's holding a fat
typescript in her hand. She snaps at MAX.*

NORMA: Stop that!

MAX stops playing.

NORMA: Today's the day.

JOE: What do you mean?

NORMA: Max is going to deliver the script to Paramount.

JOE: You're really going to give it to DeMille?

NORMA: I've just spoken to my astrologer. She read DeMille's
horoscope: she read mine.

JOE: Did she read the script?

NORMA: DeMille is Leo; I'm Scorpio. Mars is transiting
Jupiter and today is the day of closest conjunction.

JOE: Well, that's all right, then.

NORMA: Max.

NORMA hands the typescript to MAX.

NORMA: Make sure it goes to Mr DeMille in person.

MAX: Yes, Madame.

*He leaves the house by the front door. There's a silence:
NORMA moves up and down in a state of heightened emotion;
JOE is steeling himself to broach a difficult subject.*

JOE: Well . . .

NORMA: Great day.

JOE: It's been real interesting.

NORMA: Yes, hasn't it?

JOE: I want to thank you for trusting me with your baby.

NORMA: Not at all, it's I who should thank you.

JOE: Will you call and let me know as soon as you have
some news?

*NORMA frowns: she turns to him, her expression
bewildered.*

NORMA: Call where?

JOE: My apartment.

NORMA: You can't possibly think of leaving now, Joe.

JOE: The script is finished, Norma.

NORMA: No, Joe, it's just the beginning, it's the first draft: I
couldn't dream of letting you go, I need your support.

JOE: Well . . .

NORMA: You'll stay on full salary, of course . . .

JOE: It's not the money.

*NORMA now has a look of genuine panic on her face;
and JOE can see that some reassurance is essential.*

JOE: Of course, I'll wait until we get some sort of a reaction
from Paramount.

*He's on his feet now; and NORMA grips his hand tightly
for a moment.*

NORMA: Thank you, Joe.

*She releases his hand; and he moves off, a little shaken
by this turn of events, his expression rueful. He turns to the
audience.*

JOE: Well, Max climbed into that old foreign bus in the
garage, with its gold-plated car phones and leopard-skin
upholstery and trundled down to Paramount to hand in our
masterpiece. And I settled down to wait for the inevitable
rejection.

N I N E
. . . . T H E   H O U S E   O N   S U N S E T . . . .

MAX shows in an imposing, rather oily-looking men's outfitter, MR MANFRED, who's followed by a number of his assistants carrying armfuls of boxes and teetering heaps of clothing. As they begin to deploy around the room, setting out their wares, NORMA bustles in from the patio.

NORMA: Hurry up, the birthday boy is on his way.
   This is a surprise celebration
   I hope you've remembered everything I said
   I want to see a total transformation.

JOE wanders into the room: he stops in the doorway, startled by the unaccustomed crowd.

JOE: What's all this?

NORMA: Happy birthday, darling. Did you think we'd forgotten?

JOE: Well, I . . .

NORMA: These people are from the very best men's shop in town. I had them close it down for the day.

JOE: Norma, now listen!

NORMA: I'll leave you boys to it.

And before JOE can stop her, she's gone again. MANFRED is already circling warily, trying to assess his new customer; JOE looks at him, obviously dismayed, a hint of rebellion in his expression.

MANFRED: Happy birthday, welcome to your shopathon!

JOE: What's going on?

MANFRED: Help yourself, it's all been taken care of.
   Anyone who's anyone is dressed by me.

JOE: Well, golly gee.

MANFRED: Pick out anything you'd like a pair of.
   You just point, I'll do the rest
   I've brought nothing but the best.
   You're a very lucky writer.
   Come along now, get undressed.
   Unless I'm much mistaken
   That's a forty-two-inch chest.

JOE: I don't understand a word you're saying.

MANFRED: Well, all you need to know's the lady's paying.
   It's nice to get your just reward this time of year.

JOE: Get outa here!

MANFRED: And all my merchandise is strictly kosher.
   When you've thrown away all your old worn-out stuff,

JOE: Hey, that's enough.

MANFRED: Perhaps you'd like to model for my brochure.
   I have just the thing for you.
   Chalk-stripe suits

1ST S/MAN: in black

2ND S/MAN: or blue.

3RD S/MAN: glen plaid trousers

4TH S/MAN: cashmere sweaters

5TH S/MAN: bathing shorts for Malibu.

6TH S/MAN: Here's a patent leather lace-up
   It's a virtuoso shoe.

MANFRED: And a simply marvellous coat made of vicuna.

JOE: You know what you can do with your vicuna.

At this delicate point, NORMA saunters back into the room. Oblivious to the atmosphere, she registers only that no progress has been made.

NORMA: Come on, Joe, you haven't even started yet.

JOE: You wanna bet?

NORMA: I thought by now you'd look the height of fashion.

She turns to MANFRED.

NORMA: He always takes forever making up his mind.

And back to JOE.

NORMA: Don't be unkind.
   I thought you writers knew about compassion.

Impatient now, she plunges in among the clothes, towing MANFRED in her wake.

NORMA: I love flannel on a man.

She picks out a beautiful pale jacket.

MANFRED: This will complement his tan.

Now she's grabbing at shirts and trousers.

NORMA: We'll take two of these and four of those.

MANFRED: I'm still your greatest fan!
   Very soon now we'll have stopped him looking like an also-ran.

JOE: You're going to make me sorry that I'm staying.

NORMA: Well, all right, I'll choose, after all, I'm paying.

She picks out more and more clothes, handing them to the SALESMAN, JOE slouching sullenly behind her.

MANFRED: Evening clothes?

NORMA: I want to see your most deluxe.

JOE: Won't wear a tux.

NORMA: Of course not, dear, tuxedos are for waiters.

MANFRED: What we need are tails, a white tie and top hat.

JOE: I can't wear that.

NORMA: Joe, second-rate clothes are for second-raters.

JOE: Norma, please . . .

NORMA: Shut up, I'm rich
not some platinum blonde bitch.
I own so many apartments
I've forgotten which is which,
I have oil wells in the desert.

MANFRED whispers to JOE, trying to make him see reason.

MANFRED: What a salesman, what a pitch!

JOE bridles: he grabs MANFRED by his exquisitely cut lapel.

JOE: I understand your game and I'm not playing.

NORMA, however, restrains him, with a heartfelt appeal.

NORMA: Joe, please don't spoil the fun I get from paying.
Let me show you what clothes can do for a man.

The music changes and NORMA goes behind a clothes-rack and emerges dressed as Charlie Chaplin. Even JOE is charmed; and she finishes by taking a bow to general enthusiastic applause. Sensing her advantage now, she closes in on JOE.

NORMA: Joe, I'm sick to death of that
same old filling station shirt
and that boring baggy jacket
stained with yesterday's dessert.

JOE: I don't have to go to premières,
I'm never on display.
You seem to forget that I'm a writer,
who cares what you wear when you're a writer?

But he's clearly weakening: and now NORMA moves in for the kill.

NORMA: I care, Joe, and please don't be so mean to me.

JOE: OK, all right.

NORMA: You'll be Prince Charming at my New Year's
party.

JOE: I've been invited somewhere else on New Year's
Eve.

NORMA: But that's our night.

JOE: I always see the New Year in with Artie.

NORMA: I can't do without you, Joe, I need you.
I've sent out every single invitation.

JOE: All right, Norma, I give in.

NORMA: Of course you do.
And when they've dressed you, you'll cause a sensation.

And with this she sweeps off, up the stairs. JOE and MANFRED look at each other for a moment. Finally, JOE shrugs and spreads his arms, conceding. MANFRED snaps his fingers and the SALESMEN descend on JOE, engulfing him, so that he disappears in the scrimmage.

SALESMAN: We equip the chosen few of movieland.

MANFRED: (The latest cut.)

SALESMAN: We dress every movie star and crooner.
From their shiny toecaps to your hatband.

MANFRED: (Conceal your gut.)
You won't regret selecting the vicuna.

SALESMEN: If you needa hand to shake
if there's a girl you want to make
if there's a soul you're out to capture
or a heart you want to break
if you want the world to love you

MANFRED: you'll have to learn to take.

The SALESMEN move away from JOE, to reveal that he is now transformed, in full evening dress, white tie and tails.

SALESMEN: You must decide what part you are
portraying.

MANFRED is now more or less cheek to cheek with JOE. He leans forward with offensive intimacy; the gloves are off.

MANFRED: And certain parts are worth the lady paying.

SALESMEN: And why not have it all, the lady's paying?

BLACKOUT

TEN

THE HOUSE ON SUNSET
...ARTIE'S APARTMENT...

JOE paces uneasily in his white tie and tails, as a Palm Court trio begins playing tango music. He pauses to address the audience.

JOE: I couldn't imagine what sort of a gallery of waxworks Norma had invited to her New Year's party; but she'd certainly gone to town. I hadn't expected the place would look like Times Square.

LIGHTS UP on the little orchestra, tucked in under the stairs: the streamers, the trees in tubs, the floral arrangements, the dozens of blazing candles. MAX appears with a glass in one hand and a cocktail-shaker in the other. He pours the martini and hands it to JOE. The silence between them is somewhat oppressive; finally, when MAX returns with a tray of canapes, JOE breaks it:

JOE: So, Max, I suppose half the guests will be in wheelchairs, will they?

MAX: I wouldn't know, sir. Madame has made all the arrangements.

Suddenly, NORMA appears at the top of the stairs in a dazzling diamante evening gown with long black gloves and bird of paradise feathers in her hair. She begins a stately descent. JOE puts his glass down and applauds. MAX watches discreetly, evidently moved; he opens a bottle of champagne. JOE waits to meet her at the bottom of the stairs. He's reaching out to take her arm, when as if from nowhere, she suddenly produces a gold cigarette case and hands it to him.

NORMA: Here. Happy New Year.

JOE: Norma, I can't take this.

NORMA: Shut up. Open it. Read what it says.

JOE opens it and reads out, half-amused and half-appalled.

JOE: 'Mad about the boy'.

NORMA: Yes; and you do look absolutely divine.

JOE is touched, despite his embarrassment; he decides to give in gracefully and slips the cigarette case into his pocket.

JOE: Well, thank you.

NORMA stretches out a hand to lead JOE on to the freshly-waxed tiled dance-floor.

NORMA: I had these tiles put in, you know, because Valentino said to me, it takes tiles to tango. Come along.

JOE: No, no, not on the same floor as Valentino!

NORMA: Just follow me.

They begin to dance. After a while, NORMA snaps at JOE.

NORMA: Don't lean back like that.

JOE: It's that thing. It tickles.

NORMA pulls the feathers out of her hair and casts them aside. They resume dancing, closer this time.

NORMA: Ring out the old
ring in the new,
a midnight wish
to share with you.
Your lips are warm
my head is light;
were we alive
before tonight?

I don't need a crowded ballroom
everything I want is here
if you're with me
next year will be
the perfect year.

JOE is beginning to be aware what's happening; still, at the same time, he's caught up in the intoxication of the moment.

JOE: Before we play
some dangerous game,
before we fan
some harmless flame,
we have to ask
if this is wise
and if the game
is worth the prize.

With this wine and with this music,
how can anything be clear?
Let's wait and see
it just may be
the perfect year.

They dance.

NORMA: It's New Year's Eve
and hopes are high,
dance one year in,
kiss one goodbye.
Another chance,
another start,
so many dreams
to tease the heart.

We don't need a crowded ballroom
everything we want is here
and face to face
we will embrace
the perfect year. *(Reprise)*

She kisses him lightly as the number comes to an end. Then, as the orchestra strikes up the next piece, they move off the floor to take up the glasses of champagne which MAX has poured for them. They clink glasses and drink.

JOE: What time are they supposed to get here?

NORMA: Who?

JOE: The other guests.

NORMA: There are no other guests. Just you and me.

She leans in to kiss him again, this time more seriously. MAX half turns away, averting his eyes.

NORMA: I'm in love with you. Surely you know that.

JOE is terribly startled by this; all he can do is begin to bluster.

JOE: Norma, I'm the wrong guy for you: you need a big shot, someone with polo ponies, a Valentino . . .

NORMA: What you're trying to say is that you don't want me to love you. Is that it?

JOE doesn't answer: he looks away, avoiding her eye. Thus, it takes him completely by surprise when she slaps his face. And, before he can react, she's turned and run all the way up the stairs to vanish into her bedroom. Joe finds himself standing face to face with Max.

JOE: Max. Get me a taxi.

As MAX moves towards the phone, the house moves back a way to reveal ARTIE's apartment, a modest one-room affair, packed to the rafters with carefree young people, many of whom we have already encountered at the studio and at Schwab's. Several of the GUESTS cluster around the piano and there's a BOY with a saxophone. Others help themselves to some dangerous-looking alcoholic concoction from a punchbowl. The house at Sunset remains visible throughout.

As the new scene establishes itself, JOE encases himself in his vicuna coat.

JOE: I had to get out
I needed
to be with people my own age,
to hear the sound of laughter
and mix with hungry actors,
under-employed composers,
nicotine-poisoned writers,
real people,
real problems,
having a really good time.

JOE hesitates in the doorway of the apartment, suddenly embarrassed by how over-dressed he is. Meanwhile, ARTIE hails him and pushes through the crowd to greet him.

ARTIE: Hey, Gillis! We'd given you up.

BETTY by the piano, hears this and looks round, delighted to see JOE. By now, ARTIE has reached him.

ARTIE: Let me take your coat.

He touches the coat and reacts, surprised.

ARTIE: Jesus, Joe, what is this, mink?

He's even more surprised when the coat comes off to reveal JOE's tails.

ARTIE: Who did you borrow this from? Adolphe Menjou?

JOE: Close, but no cigar.

He gestures around the room.

JOE: It's quite a crowd.

ARTIE: I invited all the kids doing walk-ons in 'Samson and Delilah'.

BETTY: I'm glad you came. I want to talk to you.

JOE: Uh-oh.

Before she can develop this, the boys and girls around the piano launch into their song.

RICHARD A: You gotta say your New Year's resolution out loud.

DAWN: By this time next year
I'll have landed a juicy part.

STEVE: Nineteen Fifty will be my start
No more carrying spears.

MARY: I'll be discovered
my life won't ever be the same
Billy Wilder will know my name
and he'll call all the time.

KATHERINE: Till he does can one of you guys
lend her a dime?

ALISA: Just an apartment
with no roaches and no dry rot,

ANITA: where the hot water comes out hot.

BOTH: That's my Hollywood dream.

RICHARD A: Your resolution

JOANNA: is to write something that gets shot
with approximately the plot
I first had in my head.

MYRON: But you'll get rewritten
even after you're dead.

ARTIE: It's the year to begin a new life,
buy a place somewhere quiet, somewhere pretty.
When you have a young kid and a wife
then you need somewhere green far from the city.
It's a rambling old house with a big apple tree
with a swing for the kid and a hammock for me.

The mood is broken, as a number of GIRLS, dressed as the harem from 'Samson and Delilah' burst squealing out of the kitchen followed by SAMMY, wearing jodphurs and knee-length riding boots and carrying a megaphone. He adjusts his spectacles and assumes the grave, patriarchal air Cecil B DeMille.

SAMMY: Behold, my children,
it is I, Cecil B DeMille,
meeting me must be quite a thrill,

ADAM: but there's no need to kneel.

SAMMY: I guarantee you
every girl in my chorus line
is a genuine philistine

SANDY: they don't come off the shelf

SAMMY: I flew everyone in from Philistia myself.

The girls dance a kind of parody Middle-Eastern bump and grind, at the end of which 'CECIL B' raises the megaphone to his lips.

SAMMY: See, Samson and Delilah, coming soon to a theatre near you!

At which point a scantily clad 'SAMSON' rushes out of the kitchen, his waist-length wig billowing out behind him, pursued by a vampish 'DELILAH' brandishing a huge pair of kitchen scissors. In the pandemonium, JOE has gravitated towards BETTY.

SAMMY: See Samson conquer the might lion!
See Samson unmanned by the voluptuous Delilah!
See Samson pull down the temple of the Philistines!

Now my next project:
It's called 'The Greatest Show on Earth'

LIZ: three point six million dollars worth

GERARD & MARK: lots of sawdust and sex.

JOE: How's your next project?

BETTY: Sheldrake's anxious to option it
I've a feeling he smells a hit
we've got so much to do.

JOE: Betty, you're forgetting, I gave it to you.

Two BOYS from the 'Samson' company have begun a ludicrous kind of sand dance with tea-towels as loincloths and lampshades as fezzes.

Meanwhile, in the house, NORMA emerges from her room and descends the stairs, walking carefully as if holding herself together. MAX intercepts her with a glass of champagne. She lights a cigarette, inserts it in her holder-contraption and begins pacing up and down, listening to the orchestra with half an ear.

Back at ARTIE's apartment, when the dance is over, JOE turns to ARTIE and BETTY who are standing by the piano, their arms draped over each other's shoulders.

JOE: You remind me of me long ago
off the bus, full of ignorant ambition
thought I'd waltz into some studio
and achieve overnight recognition.
But an audience thinks when it's watching the
   screen
That the actors make up every word in the scene.

At the house, NORMA drifts back upstairs with her glass of champagne. MAX watches her leave, very concerned.

BETTY: I've done an outline,
but I can't write it on my own
can't we speak on the telephone?
All my evenings are free.

ARTIE: Hey, just a minute
I'm the fellow who bought the ring.

BETTY: Artie, this is a business thing
it's important to me.
You'll be on location in Clinch, Tennessee.

She turns to JOE, talking with a real intensity.

BETTY: Please make this your New Year's
   resolution for me.

The CHORUS starts up again.

ALL: By this time next year,
I will get my foot in the door
next year I know I'm going to score
an amazing success.

Cut to the moment
when they open the envelope
pass the statuette to Bob Hope
and it's my name you hear.

We'll be down on our knees
outside Grauman's Chinese
palm prints there on the street
immortality's neat!
This time next year
this time next year

we'll have nothing to fear
contracts all signed
three-picture deal
yellow brick road career
hope we're not still saying these things
this time next year.

Back in the house, MAX is seized by a sudden fear. Moving with surprising speed, he suddenly bounds up the stairs and disappears into NORMA's bedroom.

JOE: You know, I think I will be available in the New Year. In fact, I'm available right now.

He turns to ARTIE.

JOE: Where's your 'phone?

ARTIE: Under the bar.

JOE: Listen, could you put me up for a couple of weeks?

ARTIE: It just so happens we have a vacancy on the couch.

JOE: I'll take it.

He pushes across to the 'phone, picks it up and dials. He has to put a finger in his ear, because some new piece of nonsense has started up in the room.

The 'phone rings in the house. It rings for some time; then MAX appears on the landing, where there's an extension, looking unprecedentedly ramshackled and dishevelled. He picks up the receiver.

MAX: Yes?

JOE: Max, this is Mr Gillis. I want you to do me a favour.

MAX: I'm sorry, I cannot talk now, Mr Gillis.

JOE: Listen, I want you to get my old suitcase . . .

MAX: I'm sorry, I am attending to Madame.

JOE: What do you mean?

MAX: Madame found the razor in your room. And she cut her wrists.

Shock. BETTY, meanwhile has been making her way over to speak to him. She arrives by his side and is immediately aware something is wrong.

BETTY: What's the matter?

JOE stares at her as if he's never seen her before in his life. Then, abruptly, he hangs up and, to BETTY's total astonishment, he pushes across the room, disrupting the cabaret, grabs his coat from the bookshelf where ARTIE has carefully stowed it, and slams out of the apartment.

ARTIE's apartment dissolves; now it's the house again, the little orchestra still playing to the empty room. Presently MAX appears, supporting NORMA. Her wrists are heavily bandaged; she looks much older, frail and shaky. With infinite tenderness, MAX shepherds NORMA to the old sofa near the piano, out of sight of the orchestra. He's made the necessary preparations beforehand and now he drops to his knees and begins to bathe her forehead and temples with a flannel dipped in iced water.

Suddenly, JOE bursts through the front door, panting and extremely agitated. MAX rises; NORMA half sits up, glaring at JOE.

NORMA: Go away.

JOE: What kind of a silly thing was that to do?

NORMA: I'll do it again! I'll do it again! I'll do it again!

JOE: Attractive headline: great star kills herself for unknown writer.

NORMA: Great stars have great pride.

She turns away from him. MAX, still anxious, is moving back, melting into the background.

NORMA: You must have some girl; why don't you go to her?

Now JOE kneels beside NORMA and speaks to her with great gentleness.

JOE: I never meant to hurt you, Norma. You've been good to me. You're the only person in this stinking town that's ever been good to me.

NORMA: Then why don't you say thank you and go? Go, go!

JOE goes to the stairs as if to leave. The orchestra segues into 'Auld Lang Syne'. JOE goes to NORMA.

JOE: Happy New Year.

She reaches up and wraps her bandaged arms around his neck.

NORMA: Happy New Year, darling.

JOE leans forward, they kiss. He takes her bodily in his arms and carries her up the staircase. The orchestra plays on. MAX watches from the shadows, his expression grave and inscrutable, as JOE carries NORMA into her bedroom.

THROUGH THIS, SLOW FADE TO BLACK

INTERVAL

ACT TWO

ELEVEN
.... THE HOUSE ON SUNSET....

JOE, in sunglasses, sipping a California cocktail, sits on a chaise-longue, in the shade of a large umbrella. He smiles smugly and addresses the audience.

JOE: Sure, I came out here
to make my name
wanted my pool, my dose of fame
wanted my parking space at Warner's.

But, after a year
a one-room hell
a Murphy bed
a rancid smell
wallpaper peeling at the corners.

Sunset Boulevard
twisting Boulevard
secretive and rich, a little scary.

Sunset Boulevard
tempting Boulevard
waiting there to swallow the unwary.

Dreams are not enough
to win a war
out here they're always keeping score
beneath the tan the battle rages.

Smile a rented smile
fill someone's glass
kiss someone's wife
kiss someone's ass
we do whatever pays the wages.

Sunset Boulevard
headline Boulevard
getting here is only the beginning.

Sunset Boulevard
jackpot Boulevard
once you've won you have to go on winning.

You think I've sold out?
Dead right I've sold out.
I've just been waiting
for the right offer:
comfortable quarters,
regular rations,
twenty-four-hour
five-star room service.

And if I'm honest
I like the lady.
I can't help being
touched by her folly.
I'm treading water,
taking the money,
watching her sunset . . .
well, I'm a writer.

LA's changed a lot
over the years
since those brave gold rush pioneers
came in their creaky covered wagons.

Far as they could go
end of the line.
Their dreams were yours
their dreams were mine
but in those dreams
were hidden dragons.

Sunset Boulevard
frenzied Boulevard
swamped with every kind of false emotion.

Sunset Boulevard
brutal Boulevard
just like you we'll wind up in the Ocean.

She was sinking fast
I threw a rope
now I have suits
and she has hope
it seemed an elegant solution.

One day this must end,
it isn't real
still, I'll enjoy
a hearty meal
before tomorrow's execution.

Sunset Boulevard
ruthless Boulevard
destination for the stony-hearted.

Sunset Boulevard
lethal Boulevard
everyone's forgotten how they started
here on Sunset Boulevard.

He pours himself a glass of champagne from an open bottle. As he's sipping at it, NORMA comes hurrying out of the house in a state of high excitement.

NORMA: There's been a call
what did I say?
They want to see
me right away.
Joe, Paramount,
they love our child
Mr DeMille
is going wild.

JOE is a little surprised by this; but manages to conceal his scepticism almost at once.

JOE: Well, that's wonderful, Norma.

NORMA: But it was some fool assistant
not acceptable at all.
If he wants me, then Cecil B
himself must call.

JOE shakes his head, a little disapproving.

JOE: I don't know if this is a time to stand on ceremony.

NORMA: I've been waiting twenty years now
what's a few more days, my dear?
It's happened, Joe,
I told you so:
the perfect year.

She stretches out her hand to him, invitingly.

NORMA: Now let's go upstairs.

JOE: Don't you think you should at least call back?

NORMA: No: they can wait until I'm good and ready.

TWELVE
. . . . O N   T H E   R O A D . . . .

JOE: (V.O.) It took her three days
and she was ready
she checked with her astrologer,
who sacrificed a chicken.
She dressed up like a pharaoh,
slapped on a pound of make-up
and set forth in her chariot.
Poor Norma,
so happy,
re-entering her kingdom.

THIRTEEN
. . . . P A R A M O U N T . . . .

The Isotta-Fraschini turns up off Bronson and pulls up in front of the main gates. For the moment, nothing happens; but MAX, it emerges, is engaged in important business, staring fixedly into the rear view mirror.

MAX: (V.O.) If you will pardon me, Madame, the shadow over the left eye is not quite balanced.

NORMA: (V.O.) Thank you, Max.

She attends to it, using a handkerchief. Meanwhile MAX sounds the horn impatiently. A young STUDIO GUARD breaks off the conversation he's been having with an extra dressed as an Indian brave.

GUARD: Hey, that's enough of that.

MAX: To see Mr DeMille. Open the gate.

GUARD: Mr DeMille is shooting. You need an appointment.

MAX: This is Norma Desmond. No appointment is necessary.

GUARD: Norma who?

Meanwhile, however, NORMA has recognized JONES, who's sitting on a wooden chair, reading a newspaper. She rolls down the window.

NORMA: (offstage) Jonesy!

JONES looks up, frowning: then his expression clears.

JONES: Why, if it isn't Miss Desmond. How have you been Miss Desmond?

NORMA: (offstage) Fine, Jonesy. Open the gate.

JONES turns to his young colleague.

JONES: You heard Miss Desmond.

GUARD: They don't have a pass.

JONES shakes his head, exasperated; and opens the barrier himself. The car moves forward.

JONES: Stage Eighteen, Miss Desmond.

NORMA: (*offstage*) Thank you, Jonesy. And teach your friend some manners. Tell him without me there wouldn't be any Paramount Studio.

JONES: Get me Stage Eighteen, I have a message for Mr DeMille.

A scene-change reveals the cavernous interior of Sound Stage Eighteen, where the stand-ins for Victor Mature and Hedy Lamarr are in position, in a blaze of light, on the grandiose 'Samson and Delilah' set. Mr DeMille, recognizable from the parody version of Act I, confers with his director of photography. He's interrupted by one of his assistants, HEATHER, who approaches with some trepidation.

HEATHER: Mr DeMille?

DeMILLE: What is it?

HEATHER: Norma Desmond is here to see you, Mr DeMille.

DeMILLE: Norma Desmond?

HEATHER: She's here at the studio.

DeMILLE: It must be about that appalling script of hers. What shall I say?

HEATHER: Maybe I could give her the brush.

DeMILLE: Thirty million fans have given her the brush. Isn't that enough? Give me a minute.

He turns back towards the set.

Meanwhile, NORMA has arrived outside the studio with MAX and JOE. She hesitates for a moment gripping JOE's hand fiercely.

NORMA: Won't you come along, darling?

JOE shakes his head.

JOE: It's your script. It's your show. Good luck.

NORMA: Thank you, darling.

By this time, HEATHER, has emerged from the studio. She comes over to greet NORMA.

HEATHER: Miss Desmond.

She leads NORMA into the studio. DeMILLE is waiting just inside; he envelops her in his arms.

DeMILLE: Well, well, well.

NORMA: Hello, Mr DeMille.

A long embrace.

NORMA: Last time I saw you was someplace terribly gay. I was dancing on a table.

DeMILLE: A lot of people were. Lindbergh had just landed.

He starts to lead her into the studio.

NORMA: You read the script, of course.

DeMILLE: Well, yes . . .

NORMA: I know how busy you are when you're shooting, but I do think you could have picked up the 'phone yourself, instead of leaving it to some assistant.

DeMILLE: I don't know what you mean, Norma.

NORMA: Yes, you do.

DeMILLE: Come on in.

He leads her into the studio: a bewildering chaos of activity which at first stuns her.

He hurries off. Slowly as NORMA looks around, the sound fades to nothing. She stands there, looking around the old familiar space. Suddenly, a VOICE rings out.

VOICE: Miss Desmond! Hey, Miss Desmond!

NORMA looks around, unable to identify the source of the VOICE.

VOICE: Up here, Miss Desmond: it's Hog-eye!

NORMA looks up: up in the flies, balanced on the walkway, is a quite elderly electrician.

NORMA: Hog-eye! Well, hello!

HOG-EYE: Let's get a look at you.

And so saying, he swivels one of the big lamps until it finds her. She stands for a moment, isolated, bathed in light. Then, murmuring among themselves, from all over the studio, technicians, extras and stagehands, begin to converge on her.

NORMA: I don't know why I'm frightened,
I know my way around here
the cardboard trees,
the painted seas,
the sound here.
Yes, a world to rediscover
but I'm not in any hurry
and I need a moment.

The whispered conversations
in over-crowded hallways
the atmosphere
as thrilling here
as always.
Feel the early morning madness
feel the magic in the making
why, everything's as if we never said goodbye.

I've spent so many mornings
just trying to resist you
I'm trembling now
you can't know how
I've missed you,
missed the fairy-tale adventures
in this ever-spinning playground,
we were young together.

I'm coming out of make-up
the lights already burning
not long until
the cameras will
start turning
and the early morning madness
and the magic in the making
yes, everything's as if we never said goodbye.

I don't want to be alone
that's all in the past
this world's waited long enough
I've come home at last.

And this time will be bigger
and brighter than we knew it
so watch me fly
we all know I
can do it.
Could I stop my hand from shaking?
Has there ever been a moment
with so much to live for?

The whispered conversations
in over-crowded hallways
so much to say
not just today
but always
we'll have early morning madness
we'll have magic in the making.
Yes, everything's as if we never said goodbye.
Yes, everything's as if we never said goodbye.

We taught the world new ways to dream.

The studio staff burst into spontaneous applause.

The focus shifts to outside the studio, where JOE has moved off to lean against a wall, smoke a cigarette and enjoy the passing parade. Suddenly he sees BETTY hurrying past, a bundle of scripts under her arm. He grinds out his cigarette and steps forward to intercept her, surprising her considerably.

JOE: Hi there, Betty.

BETTY: What are you doing?

JOE: I'm out here for a meeting.

BETTY: Where have you been keeping yourself?

JOE: Someone's been doing it for me.

BETTY: We should talk.

JOE: Gotta run.

BETTY: Hold it, Joe.
I can't write this,
on my own
I thought you said you'd help me.

JOE: I'm really sorry
New Year's crisis.
Would you believe a sick friend?
It's just not
a good time,
not right now.

BETTY: Well when is a good time?

JOE: I will call you, I promise.

BETTY looks at him for a moment.

BETTY: I guess I'll have to trust you.

JOE: Thanks. I won't let you down.

BETTY smiles at him and hurries on.

During all this, SHELDRAKE has entered. He stops, having caught sight of the Isotta. He tries to catch MAX's attention, but MAX deliberately ignores him. Finally SHELDRAKE plants himself unavoidably in front of him.

SHELDRAKE: Don't you work for Norma Desmond? A couple of weeks ago I was looking out of my office window and I saw you driving onto the lot. And I said that's exactly the car I've been looking for. Great for my Crosby picture. So I made some enquiries and I've been calling for two weeks. Doesn't she ever answer the 'phone?

MAX: Go away.

SHELDRAKE: It's so perfect, you don't find that kind of thing outside of a museum. And we'll pay. I plan to offer her . . . hundred dollars a week.

MAX: Go away.

SHELDRAKE: What are you, crazy?

MAX: It's just not a good time,
not right now . . .

SHELDRAKE hurries off.

In the studio, DeMILLE has been attempting to set up his shot. Now, however, unable to ignore the kerfuffle surrounding NORMA, he steps down and approaches her; NORMA turns to him, radiant.

NORMA: Did you see
how they all came
crowding around?
They still love me
and soon we'll be
breaking new ground.
Brave pioneers.

DeMILLE: Those were the days.

NORMA: Just like before.

DeMILLE: We had such fun.

NORMA: We'll give the world
new ways to dream.

BOTH: We always found
new ways to dream.

The red light goes on and the studio bell strikes. VICTOR MATURE and HEDY LAMARR arrive to take the place of their identically costumed stand-ins.

DeMILLE: Let's have a good long talk one day.

NORMA: The old team will be back in business.

DeMILLE: Sorry, my next shot's ready.

He begins to walk her towards the studio door. Meanwhile, outside, JOE has moved over towards MAX and notices right away, from the latter's thunderous expression, that something disturbing has happened.

MAX: Mr Gillis . . .

JOE: What's the matter, Max?

MAX: I just found out the reason for all those 'phone calls from Paramount. It's not Madame they want. It's her car.

JOE: Oh, my God.

DeMILLE and NORMA have reached the doorway of the studio.

NORMA: Now, you remember, don't you? I don't work before 10 or after 4.30 in the afternoon.

DEMILLE: It isn't entirely my decision Norma, New York must be consulted.

NORMA: That's fine. You ask any exhibitor in the country. I'm not forgotten.

DEMILLE: Of course you're not.

He embraces her.

DEMILLE: Goodbye, young fellow. We'll see what we can do.

NORMA: I'm not worried. It's so wonderful to be back.

She turns and sweeps into the car, the door of which MAX is already holding open. DeMILLE waves goodbye to her; then, as the Isotta drives off, he shakes his head, disturbed, and moves, preoccupied, back into the studio. HEATHER is waiting for him.

HEATHER: Was that really Norma Desmond?

DEMILLE: It was.

HEATHER: She must be about a million years old.

DEMILLE: I hate to think where that puts me. I could be her father.

HEATHER: I'm sorry, Mr DeMille.

The shot is ready: and everyone is waiting on DeMille's orders: but he pauses for a moment, in pensive mood, his hand on the back of his chair.

DEMILLE: If you could have seen
her at seventeen
when all of her dreams were new,
beautiful and strong,
before it all went wrong:
she's never known the meaning of surrender;
never known the meaning of surrender.

S L O W   F A D E   T O   B L A C K

FOURTEEN
. . . . B E T T Y ' S   O F F I C E . . . .

Night on the Paramount lot. BETTY's office is a spartan affair, one of a row of wooden cubicles suspended at first-floor level, above the darkened streets of the back lot. BETTY sits behind her desk, staring at her typewriter, from which a piece of paper protrudes; JOE, in his shirt-sleeves, paces up and down, holding a pencil. Presently, as the silence extends, he crosses to look down at the sheet of paper in his typewriter, frowns; then, his brow clears as an idea occurs to him.

JOE: How about
they don't know each other
he works the night shift
and she takes classes all day?

Here's the thing,
they both share the same room
sleep in the same bed
it works out cheaper that way.

BETTY: Well, I've a feeling you're just kidding
but to me it sounds believable
makes a better opening than that
car chase scene:

girl finds boy
borrowing her toothbrush
or over-sleeping
or at her sewing-machine.

She's got up as the excitement over her ideas has gripped her; and now JOE takes her place behind her typewriter.

JOE: It's not bad, there are some real possibilities . . .

BETTY picks up JOE's cigarette case, helps herself to a cigarette and then notices the inscription.

BETTY: Who's Norma?

JOE: Who's who?

BETTY: I'm sorry, I don't usually read private cigarette cases.

JOE: Norma's a friend of mine, middle-aged lady, very foolish, very generous.

BETTY: I'll say: this is solid gold. 'Mad about the boy'?

JOE rises to his feet, thinks of a way to change the subject.

JOE: How's Artie?

BETTY: Stuck in Tennessee. It rains all the time, they're weeks behind. Nobody knows when they'll get back.

JOE: Good.

BETTY: What's good about it? I'm missing him something fierce.

JOE: No, I mean this idea we had is really pretty good.

He picks up the notebook, scribbles a note, as BETTY moves back towards the desk.

JOE: Back to work.

BETTY: What if *he's* a teacher?

JOE: Where does that get us?
Don't see what good it would do.

BETTY: No, it's great,
if they do the same job

JOE: so much in common
they fall in love, wouldn't you?

BETTY: Yes, but if he's just a teacher,
we lose those scenes in the factory.

JOE: Not if he's a champion for the working man.
Girl likes boy
she respects his talent.

BETTY: Working with someone
can turn you into a fan.

JOE: This is fun,
writing with a partner.

BETTY: Yes, and it could be . . .

JOE: Helluva movie.

BETTY: Can we really do this?

BOTH: I know that we can!

BLACKOUT

FIFTEEN

.... THE HOUSE ON SUNSET ....

The drawing room, gloomy and cavernous as ever. JOE sits under one of the lamps, reading a book. NORMA, her face invisible, lies face-down on the massage-table, covered only by a towel. A giant MASSEUR is working on her legs; an immaculate BEAUTICIAN, a blonde, is attending to her cuticles; and a woman ASTROLOGER in a headscarf hovers about the top end of the table.

ASTROLOGER: I don't think you should shoot
before July 15th.
Right now is a perilous time
for Pisces.
If you wait 'til Venus is in
Capricorn
you'll avoid a catalogue of crises.

The MASSEUR drums away at her thighs.

MASSEUR: I need three more weeks to get
these thighs in shape
no more carbohydrates,
don't be naughty,
we'll soon have you skipping
like an ingenue
you won't look a day over forty.

At this point, NORMA turns her face to look downstage and we see that it's coated in some thick white gunk, with slices of cucumber covering her eyes. Meanwhile, JOE puts his book down, checks his watch, gets up and begins moving round the room, trying to appear casual, but evidently looking for something.

BEAUTICIAN 1: We have dry heat, we have steam

BEAUTICIAN 2: we have moisturizing cream

BEAUTICIAN 3: we have mud-packs, we have
blood-sacks,

BEAUTICIAN 2: it's a rigorous regime

ALL: not a wrinkle when you twinkle
or a wobble when you walk

BEAUTICIAN 3: of course, there's bound to
be a little suffering

ALL: eternal youth is worth a little suffering.

ANALYST: Listen to your superego not your id,
age is just another damn neurosis
I'll have you regressing back to infancy
and back into the womb under hypnosis.

DOCTOR: I inject the tissue of the foetal lamb
the formula's the one Somerset Maugham owns
just a modest course of thirty-seven shots
and you will be a heaving mass of hormones.

ALL: No more crow's feet, no more flab
no more love handles to grab
you'll be so thin they'll all think you're
walking sideways like a crab.
Nothing sagging, nothing bagging,
nothing dragging on the floor
of course, there's bound to be a little suffering
eternal youth is worth a little suffering,
of course, there's bound to be a little suffering
eternal youth is worth a little suffering,
of course, there's bound to be a little suffering
eternal youth is worth a little suffering.

With this the beauty team packs up and leaves, shown out by MAX. JOE, still looking, winds up in NORMA'S vicinity. She suddenly produces a script from under a towel.

NORMA: Is this what you're looking for, by any chance?

JOE: Why, yes.

NORMA: Whose 'phone number is this?

JOE takes the script from her, very sheepish, not answering. NORMA rises from the massage table, gathering her towel about her, peeling the cucumber slices from her eyes.

NORMA: I've been worried about the line of my throat. This woman has done wonders with it.

JOE: Good.

NORMA: And I've lost half a pound since Tuesday.

JOE: Very good.

NORMA: And now it's after nine. I'd better get to bed.

JOE: You had.

NORMA: Are you coming up?

JOE: I think I'll read a little longer.

NORMA: You went out last night, didn't you, Joe?

JOE: I went for a walk.

NORMA: You took the car.

JOE: I drove to the beach.

NORMA: Who's Betty Schaefer?

Silence. Eventually, JOE shakes his head.

JOE: Surely you don't want me to feel I'm a prisoner in this house?

NORMA: You don't understand, Joe. I'm under a terrible strain. It's been so hard I even got myself a revolver. The only thing that stopped me using it was the thought of all those people waiting to see me back on the screen. How could I disappoint them? All I ask is a little patience, a little understanding.

JOE: Norma, there's nothing to worry about, I haven't done anything.

NORMA: Of course you haven't. Good night, my darling.

She kisses him lightly, as best she can in the circumstances, and sets off upstairs, a bizarre figure in her mask and white towel. JOE waits until she's disappeared and gathers up his script. Then he turns to the audience.

JOE: I should have stayed there.
Poor Norma,
so desperate to be ready
for what would never happen.
But Betty would be waiting,
we had the script to finish
one unexpected love scene
two people
both risking
a kind of happy ending.

He slips quietly out through the French doors. As he does so, MAX, previously seen escorting the beauty team out, quite unexpectedly emerges from the shadows of some recess in the room. His expression is troubled.

FADE TO BLACK

SIXTEEN
BETTY'S OFFICE AND THE
....BACK LOT AT PARAMOUNT....

It's night again on the Paramount lot and BETTY is once again at her typewriter: but this time there's some light on the standing New York street set, which is being dressed for action the following day. JOE watches as BETTY finishes typing.

BETTY: T - H - E - E - N - D ! I can't believe it, I've finished my first script!

JOE: Stop it, you're making me feel old.

BETTY: It's exciting, though, isn't it?

JOE: How old are you, anyway?

BETTY: Twenty-two.

JOE: Smart girl.

BETTY: Shouldn't we open some champagne?

JOE: Best I can offer is a stroll to the water cooler at the end of the lot.

BETTY: Sounds good to me. (*pause*) I love the back lot here. All cardboard, all hollow, all phoney, all done with mirrors, I think I love it better than any street in the world. I spent my childhood here.

JOE: What were you, a child actress?

BETTY: No, but my family always expected me to become a great star. I had ten years of dramatic lessons, diction, dancing, everything you can think of: then the studio made me a test.

JOE: (*laughs*) That's the saddest story I ever heard.

BETTY: I was born two blocks from here. My father was head electrician at the studio until he died, and Mother still works in wardrobe.

JOE: Second generation, huh?

BETTY: Third. Grandma did stunt work for Pearl White.

As they walk down the Manhattan street, the stage begins to revolve slowly, so that they end up walking towards downstage; and the flimsy struts holding up the substantial sets are gradually revealed. JOE and BETTY walk in silence for a while; BETTY's expression is deeply preoccupied. They come to a halt in front of the water cooler.

JOE: I guess it is kind of exciting, at that, finishing a script.

He fixes a couple of paper cups of water; and hands one to BETTY, who's miles away and comes to with a start when he touches her arm.

BETTY: What?

JOE: Are you all right?

BETTY: Sure.

JOE: Something's the matter, isn't it?

Pause. Then Betty blurts out.

BETTY: I had a telegram from Artie.

JOE: Is something wrong?

BETTY: He wants me to come out to Tennessee. He says it would only cost two dollars to get married in Clinch.

JOE: Well, what's stopping you? Now we've finished the script . . .

He breaks off, amazed to see that she's crying.

JOE: Why are you crying? You're getting married, isn't that what you wanted?

BETTY: Not any more.

JOE: Don't you love Artie?

BETTY: Of course I do. I'm just not in love with him any more, that's all.

JOE: Why not? What happened?

BETTY: You did.

Suddenly, they're in each other's arms. A long kiss.

BETTY: When I was a kid,
I played on this street,
I always loved illusion.
I thought make-believe
was truer than life
but now it's all confusion
please can you tell me what's happening?
I just don't know any more.
If this is real,
how should I feel?
What should I look for?

JOE: If you were smart,
you would keep on walking
out of my life
as fast as you can.
I'm not the one
you should pin your hopes on,
you're falling for
the wrong kind of man.
This is crazy.
You know we should call it a day.
Sound advice, great advice,
let's throw it away.
I can't control
all the things I'm feeling,
I haven't got a prayer
if I'm a fool, well, I'm too much in love to care.
I knew where I was,
I'd given up hope,
made friends with disillusion.
No one in my life,
but I look at you
and now it's all confusion.

BETTY: Please can you tell me what's happening?
I just don't know any more.
If this is real,
how should I feel?
What should I look for?
I thought I had
everything I needed.
My life was set,
my dreams were in place.
My heart could see
way into the future.
All of that goes
when I see your face.
I should hate you,

there I was, the world in my hand
can one kiss kiss away
everything I planned?
I can't control
all the things I'm feeling,
I'm floating in mid-air.
I know it's wrong, but I'm too much in love to care.

BOTH: I thought I had
everything I needed.
My life was set,
my dreams were in place
my heart could see
way into the future.
All of that goes
when I see your face
this is crazy.
You know we should call it a day.

JOE: Sound advice,

BETTY: great advice,

BOTH: let's throw it away.
I can't control
all the things I'm feeling.
We're floating in mid-air.
If we are fools, well, we're too much
in love to care.
If we are fools, well, we're too much
in love to care.

They fall into each other's arms and embrace passionately. Then JOE leads BETTY by the hand back into the office. They kiss again and it's obvious that they're about to make love.

SEVENTEEN

. . . . T H E   H O U S E   O N   S U N S E T . . . .
(E X T E R I O R)

It's late at night as JOE, in the Isotta, glides back into the garage. He steps down from the car with a gleam in his eye and a spring in his step; and is therefore thoroughly startled when the sombre figure of MAX steps forward out of the darkness. However, he recovers quickly. It's a murky night, wind rising, rain threatening.

JOE: What's the matter there, Max? You waiting to wash the car?

MAX: Please be careful when you cross the patio. Madame may be watching.

JOE: Suppose I tiptoe up the back stairs and undress in the dark, will that do it?

MAX: It's just that I am greatly worried about Madame.

JOE: Well, we're not helping any, feeding her lies and more lies. What happens when she finds out they're not going to make her picture?

MAX: She never will. That is my job. I made her a star and I will never let her be destroyed.

JOE: You made her a star?

MAX: I directed all her early pictures. In those days there were three young directors who showed promise: D W Griffith, Cecil B DeMille and . . .

JOE interrupts, as the realization suddenly dawns on him.

JOE: Max von Mayerling.

MAX: That's right.

By now, they've moved out of the garage on to the dimly lit patio.

MAX: When we met
she was a child,
barely sixteen;
awkward and yet
she had an air
I'd never seen.
I knew I'd found
my perfect face.
Deep in her eyes,
new ways to dream,
and we inspired
new ways to dream.

Talkies came:
I stayed with her,
took up this life,
threw away fame.

He hesitates, before steeling himself to go on.

Please understand

A beat.

she was my wife.

Pause. JOE is staggered. MAX is fighting back a wave of emotion.

We had achieved
far more than most
we gave the world
new ways to dream.
Everyone needs
new ways to dream.

JOE shakes his head, still incredulous.

JOE: You're telling me you were married to her?

MAX: I was the first husband.

EIGHTEEN

. . . . T H E   H O U S E   O N   S U N S E T . . . .
(INTERIOR)

The main room comes into view: and NORMA, her face now bare of make-up, wearing a black negligee, her expression profoundly tormented, picks up the phone and dials.

NORMA: Hello, is this Gladstone 9281? Miss Schaefer? . . . Miss Schaefer, you must forgive me for calling so late, but I really feel it's my duty. It's about Mr Gillis . . . .You do know a Mr Gillis? Well, exactly how much do you know about him? Do you know where he lives? Do you know what he lives on?

At around this point, JOE, unseen by NORMA, steps in through the front door and freezes in the shadows, listening.

NORMA: I want to spare you
a lot of sadness.
I don't know what he's told you,
but I can guarantee you
he doesn't live with mother
or what you'd call a roommate.
He's just a . . . I can't say it.
Poor Betty
you ask him,
I'd love to hear his answer.

She's completely taken by surprise, as JOE snatches the receiver from her.

JOE: That's right, Betty, why don't you ask me? Or better yet, come over and see for yourself. Yes, right now. The address is ten-thousand-eighty-six, Sunset Boulevard.

He hangs up violently and turns to stare at NORMA in furious silence. She flinches under his gaze.

NORMA: Don't hate me, Joe. I did it because I need you. Look at me. Look at my hands. Look at my face. Look under my eyes. How can I go back to work if I'm wasting away?

JOE says nothing; he's trying to control his rage.

NORMA: Don't stand there hating me, Joe. Shout at me, strike me, but say you don't hate me.

But JOE who has been looking at her with an expression of infinite contempt, deliberately turns his back on her.

A distant rumble of thunder: an orchestral INTERLUDE begins, during which the storm intensifies, a torrential tropical rain starts to fall, lightning flashes and NORMA makes her way shakily up the stairs. JOE paces, steeling himself for the coming encounter. NORMA vanishes into her bedroom, JOE finally slumps on the big sofa. Unseen by him, NORMA re-emerges, quietly, on to the landing: she's holding a revolver. She sinks to the floor and waits.

The shrill of the doorbell. JOE, alone in the great room, springs to his feet and hurries to let BETTY in.

JOE: Come on in.

He leads BETTY into the main room. She looks around for a moment, unnerved by the size of the place.

BETTY: What's going on, Joe?
Why am I so scared?
What was that woman saying?
She sounded so weird,
I don't understand . . .

Please can't you tell me what's happening?
Don't you love me any more?
Shall I just go?
Say something, Joe.

NORMA moves stealthily forward, staring down at BETTY through the balustrade.

JOE: Have some pink champagne
and caviar
when you go visit with a star,
the hospitality is stellar.

BETTY: So this is where you're living?

JOE: Yes, it's quite a place
  sleeps seventeen
  eight sunken tubs
  a movie screen
  a bowling alley in the cellar.

BETTY: I didn't come to see a house, Joe.

JOE: Sunset Boulevard
  cruise the Boulevard
  win yourself a Hollywood palazzo.

  Sunset Boulevard
  mythic Boulevard
  Valentino danced on the terrazzo.

BETTY: Who's it belong to?

JOE: Just look around you.

BETTY: That's Norma Desmond.

She's seen the big portrait above the fireplace; now JOE begins to draw her attention to some of the innumerable other portraits, photographs and stills.

JOE: Right on the money
  that's Norma Desmond
  that's Norma Desmond
  that's Norma Desmond
  that's Norma Desmond.

BETTY: Why did she call me?

JOE: Give you three guesses.
  It's the oldest story
  in the book:
  come see the taker being took
  the world is full of Joes and Normas.

  Older woman
  very well-to-do
  meets younger man
  a standard cue
  for two mechanical performers.

BETTY puts a hand over his mouth.

BETTY: Just pack your things and let's go.

JOE: You mean *all* my things?
  Have you gone mad?
  Leave all the things I've never had?
  Leave this luxurious existence?

  You want me to face
  that one-room hell,
  that Murphy bed,
  that rancid smell,
  go back to living on subsistence?

  It's no time to begin a new life,
  now I've finally made a perfect landing.
  I'm afraid there's no room for a wife,
  not unless she's uniquely understanding.
  You should go back to Artie and marry the fool
  and you'll always be welcome to swim in my pool.

BETTY: I can't look at you any more, Joe.

She turns and rushes blindly out of the French door, leaving it open. Wind and rain. JOE's head slowly sinks; he's overcome by a wave of misery. Meanwhile, on the landing, NORMA scrambles to her feet. The revolver is no longer in evidence. She crosses the landing and starts off down the stairs: a flutter of movement catches JOE's eye and he turns. NORMA stops on the stairs, temporarily halted by the fierceness of his expression, but as he moves towards her and starts up the stairs, she stretches out a hand to him.

NORMA: Thank you, thank you, Joe, thank you.

JOE brushes past her, brusquely shaking off her hand as she touches his wrist and vanishing into his room. She stays where she is, uncertain, unable to make sense of what's happening; and, suddenly, JOE reappears. He's carrying his battered old typewriter. Calm and unhurried, he starts off down the stairs again, as NORMA stares wildly at him.

NORMA: What are you doing, Joe?

He ignores her, continues to move evenly down the stairs.

NORMA: You're not leaving me?

JOE: Yes, I am, Norma.

NORMA: You can't! Max! Max!

JOE: It's been a bundle of laughs
  and thanks for the use of the trinkets.

He takes the gold cigarette case out of his pocket and hands it to her.

JOE: A little ritzy for the copy desk
  back in Dayton.

He starts to move on, then turns back to her, his expression serious.

  And there's something you ought to know.
  I want to do you this favour:
  they'll never shoot that hopeless
    script of yours.
  They only wanted your car.

During this, MAX has entered, below. He looks on, helpless.

NORMA: That's a lie! They still want me!
  What about all my fan mail?

JOE: It's Max who writes you letters.
  Your audience has vanished.
  They left when you weren't looking.
  Nothing's wrong with being fifty
  unless you're acting twenty.

He sets off down the stairs.

NORMA: I'm the greatest star of them all.

JOE: Goodbye, Norma.

He's spoken without looking back; so he doesn't see NORMA fetch the revolver out of her pocket and point it at him.

NORMA: No one ever leaves a star.

She fires. JOE looks extremely surprised, but carries on walking, for the moment apparently unaffected. At the bottom of the stairs, he lets go of the typewriter, which crashes down on to the tiles. He staggers slightly, but carries on, out through the French door. NORMA hurries after him. Outside the door, she fires twice more. A flash of lightning is followed by a drum roll of thunder. MAX moves forward to the centre of the stage, aghast, for once completely at a loss.

SLOW FADE TO BLACK

NINETEEN
.... THE HOUSE ON SUNSET ....

In the BLACKOUT, the orchestra plays NORMA's 'Lullaby', and soon the LIGHTS come up on the cold dawn of the opening scene. There's been a semi-revolve, so that the garden is now visible, bathed in an eerie glow, disrupted by the blue lights of the patrol cars. JOE's body floats, face-down, in the pool. The entrance hall of the house is crowded with reporters, police, newsreel crews with their cameras, all fired with eager anticipation. MAX moves around the various groups, consulting with policemen and cameramen.

JOURNALIST: *(on the 'phone)* As day breaks over the murder house Norma Desmond, famed star of yesteryear, is in a state of complete mental shock.

Suddenly, all movement stops and all heads rise: NORMA has emerged from her room on to the landing. She's dressed in some strange approximation of a Salome costume and she's still holding the revolver. There's an atmosphere of extreme apprehension below. One of the uniformed POLICEMEN has brought out his gun; MAX leans over to talk to the head of Homicide, a plainclothes detective. She's clearly disorientated, in a world of her own, moving, lost and bewildered, around the landing, letting out, unaccompanied by the orchestra, old broken phrases.

NORMA: This was dawn.
I don't know why I'm frightened.
Silent music starts to play.
Happy New Year, darling.
If you're with me, next year will be . . .
Next year will be . . .
They bring in his head on a silver tray.
She kisses his mouth . . .
She kisses his mouth . . .
Mad about the boy!
They'll say Norma's back at last!

MAX: Madame, the cameras have arrived.

NORMA: Max, where am I?

MAX: This is the staircase of the palace
and they're waiting for your dance.

NORMA: Of course,
now I remember:
I was so frightened I might fall . . .

MAX: You are the greatest star of all!

She starts down the stairs; MAX cups a hand to his mouth and springs into action.

MAX: Lights!

The portable lights flare up. In addition, there's the flash of countless flashbulbs. NORMA reacts, her eyes widen, she drapes the scarf around her shoulders.

MAX: Cameras!

The whirr and grind of the old-fashioned Movietone cameras.

MAX: Action!

And so, as the music swells, NORMA descends the staircase, waving her arms in some strange rendition of Salome's approach to the throne. However, half-way down, she suddenly comes to a halt and begins to speak.

NORMA: I can't go on with the scene: I'm too happy.
May I say a few words, Mr DeMille?
I can't tell you how wonderful it is to be back in the studio making a picture. I promise you I'll never desert you again.

**I've spent so many mornings
just trying to resist you
I'm trembling now
you can't know how
I've missed you,
could I stop my hand from shaking?
Has there ever been a moment
with so much to live for?**

This is my life. It always will be. There is nothing else. Just us and the cameras and all your wonderful people out there in the dark. And now, Mr DeMille, I'm ready for my close-up.

She continues down the staircase as 'With One Look' swells to a climax.

**This time I'm staying
I'm staying for good
I'll be back
where I was born to be
with one look
I'll be me.**

DARKNESS

THE END

1. First light on Sunset Boulevard. A convoy of police cars and motorcycles races along the otherwise deserted street and turns into a driveway, pulling up by a swimming pool in which a man's body is floating. The corpse narrates; he is Joe Gillis, a hard-up screenwriter.

2. Flashback to six months earlier at the Alta-Nido building in Hollywood. Joe is sitting in his one-room apartment typing. Two men arrive to repossess his car but he tells them he has lent it. They warn that it must be back by the following day.

3. Joe retrieves his car from its hiding place in a nearby parking lot and drives to Paramount Studios.

4. He tries to interest a producer, Sheldrake, in a baseball screenplay he sent to the studio some time earlier. Sheldrake calls for a report on it. The reader, Betty Schaefer, enters and says that the story is bad. Sheldrake introduces her to its author and she is abashed. Sheldrake sends Joe away empty-handed.

5. At Schwab's drugstore Joe makes calls to try to raise money, without success.

6. He meets his agent on the Bel-Air golf course who adamantly refuses to help.

7. The angry Joe, while driving back on Sunset, is spotted by the repossession men in another car, and they give chase. On a curve Joe has a blow out and pulls into a hidden driveway, eluding his pursuers. He parks his car in an open garage and notes a much older, expensive limousine on blocks. As he walks away a woman calls him from the upper floor of the adjacent mansion, and a butler, Max, motions him from the doorway to enter, observing that he is inappropriately dressed.

8. Joe is ushered into the presence of Norma Desmond, who thinks that he has come to arrange the funeral of her pet monkey. When she learns that he is an accidental visitor she throws him out. He then recognizes her as a former silent movie star.

9. On his way down the grand staircase he is stopped by her. She has registered that he is a writer, and proposes that he helps to shape her script of Salome, with which she hopes to return to films. In the drawing-room he is given the huge draft to read

and decides to take advantage of the suggestion in order to make some money. He is told to stay the night in a room over the garage.

10. Max shows him to the room. Later as Joe looks out of the window he sees Max and Norma conducting the pet's funeral in the garden. He wakes next day to find his possessions have been brought over.

11. Joe enters the main house where Max is playing the organ. He tells Joe that his rent arrears have been settled. Norma tells him to work on the script.

12. Days pass while he knocks the hopeless script into a semblance of an acceptable screenplay. In an interlude Max projects one of Norma's old films.

13. During a bridge session in which Norma is playing with three of her silent-screen contemporaries Joe is told by Max that the repossessors have found his car. He interrupts the game to ask Norma to lend him money but she refuses, and the car is towed away.

14. Max has put Norma's Isotta-Fraschini back on the road and chauffeurs her on a drive with Joe.

15. In a menswear shop Norma outfits Joe in better clothes. A salesman suggests he takes vicuna rather than camelhair because it is not he who is footing the bill.

16. Rain leaks through the ceiling of the room over the garage and Max moves Joe to the main house.

17. Joe is given the bedroom formerly used by Norma's husbands. He notes there are no doorlocks and Max tells him that there are none in the house, all removed because of Norma's suicide attempts.

18. New Year's Eve. Joe, immaculate in tails, descends the stairs to attend Norma's party. She greets him and whisks him into a tango. There is nobody else there, apart from Max and the band. Norma tells him that the party is for him alone. There is a quarrel and Joe storms off into the night.

19. The apartment of Joe's best friend, Artie, is crowded with revellers, and Joe in tails looks out-of-place. He meets Betty, discovering that she is Artie's fiancée. She tells Joe that she has found another of his scripts that she thinks would be worthwhile after

work on it and wants to help. Joe, delighted to be back with his own age group, decides to move in with Artie. He telephones Max to have his clothes sent over. Max tells him that Norma has slashed her wrists, and Joe abruptly leaves the noisy party.

20. At the mansion he finds Norma with bandaged wrists. There is now no question of leaving her.

21. Betty a few days later phones Joe, but Max refuses to pass on the call and orders her not to ring again. Joe, unaware, is at the swimming pool with Norma.

22. On a nocturnal excursion in the limousine Joe asks to stop at Schwab's to buy cigarettes. He runs into Artie and Betty. She renews her enthusiasm for working with him, and suggests that they can do it while Artie is away on location. The conversation is interrupted by Max who points out that madam is waiting.

23. Norma entertains Joe with impersonations of a Mack Sennett bathing beauty and Charlie Chaplin. Max intervenes to tell her that Paramount have called, and she assumes that DeMille wants to see her.

24. Norma's car arrives at the studio gate, but an officious young guard refuses entry until put in his place by an older one who remembers her heyday.

25. The set of Cecil B DeMille's *Samson and Delilah*. The director has been told that Norma is visiting and goes to the door of the sound stage to greet her. An old-timer lighting grip recognizes her and shines a spotlight, and an admiring crowd gathers. DeMille handles her tactfully.

26. Joe while talking to Max outside spots Betty and runs after her.

27. In Betty's office he and she talk about their possible script collaboration, but Max calls him away and says that he has learned that it is the car that the studio is interested in, not Norma. They resolve that she must not find out.

28. Norma, believing she will soon be back before the cameras, embarks on extensive beauty treatments.

29. At night in Betty's office Joe and she are secretly working on their screenplay. Betty finds his expensive cigarette case, a gift from Norma, and is curious.

30. Joe and Betty walk the deserted Paramount backlot at night, and fall in love.

31. Joe, stealthily returning to Norma's mansion finds Max waiting in the garage, telling him that she is aware of his clandestine outings, and he is concerned for her. He reveals that he was her first director and first husband.

32. Norma finds Joe and Betty's script, with Betty's name and phone number.

33. Betty in another late-night work session tells Joe that she is going to ditch Artie for him.

34. Joe returns to the house determined to break with Norma.

35. Norma in her bedroom is telephoning Betty and attempting to explain her relationship with Joe. He enters and realizing what she is doing takes the phone, confirming the truth and inviting Betty to come over and see for herself.

36. Betty arrives at the house and Joe harshly tells her what has happened, and sends her out of his life.

37. As he is packing his suitcase to leave her Norma pleads with him to stay. He refuses, and begins to walk down the stairs and out of the house. Norma shoots him three times. He topples into the swimming pool, dead.

38. A return to the scene at the beginning as the body, watched by policemen, reporters and photographers, is fished from the pool.

39. In Norma's bedroom the police are anxious to get her downstairs and into custody, but the situation is fraught. Max offers to help, and tells Norma that the cameras are ready.

40. Norma, now completely insane, glides down the staircase, believing that she is at last playing Salome for Cecil B DeMille.

ACKNOWLEDGEMENTS

There are many people who have encouraged and helped me in preparing this book, not least of whom is Billy Wilder, the creator of *Sunset Boulevard*. Throughout the complex and occasionally tense process of translating a great film into a stage musical Sir Andrew Lloyd Webber unhesitatingly gave me his time and confidence without ever imposing his views over mine. Others in the creative team, especially Don Black, Christopher Hampton, Trevor Nunn, John Napier and Anthony Powell were always frank and helpful. Patti LuPone invited my wife and I to her home in Connecticut and became a good friend. At the Really Useful Group everyone I was in contact with went far beyond duty to help me, particularly Patrick McKenna, Keith Turner, Sue Watts, Judith Morgan and Marie Curtin. Sir Andrew Lloyd Webber's assistant, Sarah Snow, was consistently helpful as was Peter Thompson, the doyen of press representatives for West End musicals. Alan Benson, in the course of making his documentary on *Sunset Boulevard* freely shared his knowledge, John Muir, the architect in whose hands the restoration of the Adelphi Theatre rested allowed me to examine its fabric in intimate close-up. David Cheshire of the Theatres Trust gave me the historical background. In the United States I was particularly grateful to Diane Rosenkrantz, vice-president of Gloria Swanson Inc in New York, Marc Wanamaker of the Bison Archive in Los Angeles, the helpful staff of the Los Angeles City Archives, particularly Hynda L. Rudd and Robert B. Freeman, the Harry Ransom Humanities Research Center,

The University of Texas at Austin, particularly Dr Tom Staley, Joan Sibley, Dr Charles Bell and Dr Roy Flukinger, Paramount Pictures, the Kobal Collection, the BFI, and to my old friends Dr Irene Kassorla and Norman Friedman in Los Angeles. The exacting publication schedule and a number of unforeseen technical obstacles did not deter the visionary drive of Colin Webb, the managing director of Pavilion Books who made publication possible. With Helen Sudell and Emma Lawson as his editorial team and Kate Thomas in production the impossible has been achieved. The calm skill of Peter Bridgewater and his team resulted in a polished design that belies the speed with which it was produced. I should also express gratitude to my agent Pat White of Rogers, Coleridge and White, and especially to my wife Frances who assisted at every stage, and to my son Matthew who discovered a great film.

GEORGE PERRY, LONDON, AUGUST 1993

The publishers wish to thank the following copyright holders for their permission to reproduce the illustrations listed below:

Paramount Pictures/The Kobal Collection p.33, 37, 41, 44, 50, 54 (left) 57, 58, 59 (top), 64; Paramount Pictures/BFI p.53 (bottom), 55 (left), 56, 61; Paramount Pictures/Marc Wanamaker, Bison Archives p.46, 49, 52, 53 54 (right), 55 (right), 59 (bottom), 62, 71 (top), 75; Paramount Pictures /Harry Ransom Humanities Research Center, The University of Texas at Austin p.60, 65, 66, 67, 70, 76; The Kobal Collection p.43; Marc Wanamaker, Bison Archives p.13, 14, 15, 17, 18, 19, 20, 21, 23, 24, 25, 26, 27, 29, 30, 31, 32,38, 39, 47, 68, 71 (bottom), 72; Harry Ransom Humanities Research Center, The University of Texas at Austin p.10, 73, 74, 79; Anthony Crickmay p.82, p.16 appeared in Happy Birthday Hollywood! (The Motion Picture and Television Fund, 1987). Production photography was by Donald Cooper and David Crosswaite. Patti LuPone costume photographs by Tony McGee.

CREATIVE TEAM

MUSIC BY **ANDREW LLOYD WEBBER**
BOOK & LYRICS BY **DON BLACK**
& CHRISTOPHER HAMPTON

Based on the Billy Wilder film
PRODUCTION DESIGNED BY **JOHN NAPIER**
COSTUMES DESIGNED BY **ANTHONY POWELL**
LIGHTING DESIGNED BY **ANDREW BRIDGE**
MUSICAL SUPERVISION & DIRECTION BY
DAVID CADDICK
SOUND DESIGNED BY **MARTIN LEVAN**
MUSICAL DIRECTOR **DAVID WHITE**
ORCHESTRATIONS BY **DAVID CULLEN**
& ANDREW LLOYD WEBBER
MUSICAL STAGING BY **BOB AVIAN**
DIRECTED BY **TREVOR NUNN**

THE ORIGINAL CAST, ORCHESTRA AND PRODUCTION CREDITS

NORMA DESMOND **PATTI LuPONE**
JOE GILLIS **KEVIN ANDERSON**
MAX VON MAYERLING **DANIEL BENZALI**
BETTY SCHAEFER **MEREDITH BRAUN**
CECIL B DeMILLE **MICHAEL BAUER**
MANFRED **NICOLAS COLICOS**
SHELDRAKE **HARRY DITSON**
ARTIE GREEN **GARETH SNOOK**

Other roles are performed by
KATE ARNEIL GERARD CASEY
ANITA LOUISE COMBE STEVE DEVEREAUX
ALISA ENDSLEY NICOLA JANE FILSHIE
PETER GALE LIZ GREENAWAY
SIMON HAYDEN MARK INSCOE
ADAM MATALON SASHA MILLARD
DAPHNE PEÑA PARDY RICHARD PURRO
BERNARD SHARPE DAWN SPENCE
NADIA STRAHAN SANDY V-STRALLEN
RICHARD TATE

UNDERSTUDIES

NORMA DESMOND **CAROL DUFFY**
JOE GILLIS **GERARD CASEY**
MAX VON MAYERLING **MICHAEL BAUER**
ARTIE GREEN **MARK INSCOE**
CECIL B DeMILLE **PETER GALE**

THE ORCHESTRA

VIOLIN 1 (LEADER) **MARTIN TURNLUND**
VIOLIN 2 **NICHOLAS MILLER**
VIOLIN 3 **JAYNE HARRIS**
VIOLIN 4 **SHELLEY VAN LOEN**
VIOLIN 5 **CLIVE HUGHES**
VIOLIN 6 **PETER McGOWEN**
VIOLIN 7 **ADRIAN DUNN**
VIOLA 1 **CATHRYN McCRACKEN**
VIOLA 2 **NIGEL GOODWIN**
CELLO **TREVOR BURLEY**
FLUTE/PICCOLO/ALTO FLUTE **DEBORAH DAVIS**
CLARINET/FLUTE/SAXOPHONE **JOHN WHELAN**
CLARINET/SAXOPHONE **NICK MOSS**
TRUMPET **NOEL LANGLEY**
HORN 1 **ROGER CLARK**
HORN 2 **HUW EVANS**
TROMBONE **STEVE WILKES**
GUITAR **MIKE EAVES**
BASS **ALLEN WALLEY**
DRUMS **JULIAN FAIRBANK**
KEYBOARD 1 **PETER LEE**
KEYBOARD 2 **PAUL HONEY**
ASSISTANT MUSICAL DIRECTOR/KEYBOARD 3
ANDREW FRIESNER

PRODUCTION

RESIDENT DIRECTOR **ANDREW MacBEAN**
ASSOCIATE CHOREOGRAPHER **MAGGIE GOODWIN**
COMPANY MANAGER **RICHARD ORIEL**
PRODUCTION STAGE MANAGER **PIPPA SHAW**
STAGE MANAGERS **STEPHEN BURNETT,**
DEBBIE CRONSHAW
ASSISTANT STAGE MANAGERS **LEE FOWLER,**
EMILY FULLER, EMMA NEIGHBOUR,
NIGEL SHILTON
HYDRAULICS OPERATOR No 1 **MIKI JABLKOWSKA**
HYDRAULICS OPERATORS **GRAHAM COFFEY,**
ROBERT POOLEY
SOUND OPERATOR No 1 **DREW MOLLISON**
SOUND OPERATOR No 2 **JULIE COLE**
SOUND OPERATOR No 3 **JANE HARRINGTON**
DANCE CAPTAIN **SANDY V-STRALLEN**
WARDROBE MASTER **JOHN SHARMAN**
DEPUTY WARDROBE MISTRESS **ALISON KANE**
WARDROBE ASSISTANT **KATE AARONS**
WIG MISTRESS **SUE STROTHER**
DEPUTY WIG MISTRESSES **JEANETTE FUSTER,**
CHRISTINE QUINNELL